An American Family

VISIBLE EVIDENCE

Edited by Michael Renov, Faye Ginsburg, and Jane Gaines

*Public confidence in the "real" is everywhere in decline. The Visible
Evidence series offers a forum for the in-depth consideration of the
representation of the real, with books that engage issues bearing upon
questions of cultural and historical representation, and that forward the
work of challenging prevailing notions of the "documentary tradition"
and of nonfiction culture more generally.*

VISIBLE EVIDENCE, VOLUME 11

An American Family

A Televised Life

Jeffrey Ruoff

 University of Minnesota Press

Minneapolis

London

Earlier versions of portions of chapter 3 appeared as "'A Bastard Union of Several Forms': Style and Narrative in *An American Family*," in *Documenting the Documentary,* edited by Barry Keith Grant and Jeannette Sloniowski (Detroit: Wayne State University Press, 1998), 286–301; copyright 1998 Wayne State University Press; reprinted with permission of Wayne State University Press. Earlier versions of parts of chapter 5 appeared as "Conventions of Sound in Documentary," *Cinema Journal* 32, no. 3 (1993): 24–40; copyright 1993 University of Texas Press; used by permission of University of Texas Press; and as "Conventions of Sound in Documentary," in *Sound Theory, Sound Practice* (a volume in the series AFI Film Readers), edited by Rick Altman (New York and London: Routledge, 1992), 217–34; copyright 1992 Routledge; reprinted by permission of Routledge. Earlier versions of parts of chapters 6 and 7 appeared as "Can a Documentary Be Made of Real Life? The Reception of *An American Family*," in *The Construction of the Viewer: Media Ethnography and the Anthropology of Audiences,* edited by Peter Ian Crawford and Sigurjón Baldur Hafsteinsson (Højbjorg: Intervention Press, 1996), 270–96; copyright 1996 Intervention Press; used by permission of Intervention Press.

Published by the University of Minnesota Press
111 Third Avenue South, Suite 290
Minneapolis, MN 55401-2520
http://www.upress.umn.edu

Library of Congress Cataloging-in-Publication Data

Ruoff, Jeffrey Kevin.
    An American family : a televised life / Jeffrey Ruoff.
        p.   cm. — (Visible evidence ; v. 11)
    Includes bibliographical references and index.
    ISBN 978-0-8166-3560-3 (HC : alk. paper)
    ISBN 978-0-8166-3561-0 (PB : alk. paper)
        1. Family—United States.   2. Middle class—United States.   3. Documentary
    television programs—United States.   4. American family (Television program)
    I. Title.   II. Series.
    HQ536 .R86 2001
    306.85'0973—dc21

                                                                                    2001003079

Printed in the United States of America on acid-free paper

The University of Minnesota is an equal-opportunity educator and employer.

15 14 13 12 11   10 9 8 7 6 5 4 3

To Philippe Roques, filmmaker

What thou lovest well remains.
:: Ezra Pound, Canto LXXXI

It is, I believe, as new and significant as the invention of drama or the novel—a new way in which people can learn to look at life, by seeing the real life of others interpreted by the camera.
::   Margaret Mead, *TV Guide*, January 6, 1973

Margaret Mead, bless her friendly voice, has written glowingly that the series constituted some sort of breakthrough, a demonstration of a new tool for use in sociology and anthropology. Having been the object of that tool, I think I am competent to say that it won't work.
::   Pat Loud, *Los Angeles Times*, March 4, 1973

Contents

Preface

The advent of satellite and cable television in the 1980s, together with intense competition among American networks for advertising revenues, left broadcast media scrambling for ways to reach audiences. Using new small-format video technologies that make taping possible under virtually any circumstances, producers have introduced a flood of inexpensive reality-based shows, often called "reality TV" or "docu-soaps." Fox's *Cops* (1989–present), which follows actual police officers while they patrol the streets of America, led the way. Subsequently, ABC's *America's Funniest Home Videos* (1990–present) brought amateur footage into prime time as studio audiences voted to award $10,000 to the evening's most amusing clip. MTV's *The Real World* (1992–present) held casting tryouts for another hybrid form in which seven youths, strangers at the outset of the show, lived together in a loft apartment specifically constructed for filming purposes. As I write this preface, CBS's *Survivor,* with its game-show format and tropical island setting, has become the hit of the summer of 2000, prompting *Time* magazine to do a cover story on "voyeur TV."[1] As audiences followed the ups and downs of the dwindling number of contestants for the million-dollar prize, *Business Week* reported that *Survivor* was "rejuvenating the network's demographics and boosting summer ratings."[2] Commercial success guarantees that programmers will offer more of the same: reality TV is designed to make real life pay.

But before "infotainment" and "reality programming," there was a nonfiction series called *An American Family.* Produced by Craig Gilbert, this documentary chronicled seven months in the lives of the Loud family of Santa Barbara, California, including the divorce proceedings of the parents and the New York lifestyle of their gay son, Lance. Twelve episodes long, *An American Family* was shown weekly on the Public Broadcasting Service in 1973; millions watched. The Louds—wife Pat, husband Bill, and their children, Lance, Kevin, Grant, Delilah, and Michele—became house-hold names. Unlike the contrived situations and game-show formats of current reality programming, the PBS documentary portrayed everyday life without embellishment. No prizes were awarded. There were no commercials, because *An American Family* was not broadcast to make money.

Producer Gilbert deliberately chose an upper-middle-class family whose lifestyle approximated that of families seen on situation comedies such as *Leave It to Beaver* (1957–63) and *The Adventures of Ozzie & Harriet* (1952–66). As in *The Brady Bunch* (1969–74), there were plenty of kids in the family. But by the time Pat Loud asked her husband to move out of the house in the ninth episode, the old ideal of carefree sitcom families had crumbled. Gilbert's use of narrative techniques in a nonfictional account of family life blurred conventions of different media forms. Unlike most documentaries, *An American Family* had no host, no interviews, and no voice-over narration. By bringing cameras into the home, *An American Family* announced the breakdown of fixed distinctions between public and private, reality and spectacle, serial narrative and nonfiction, documentary and fiction, film and television.

It is worth revisiting this groundbreaking documentary today because it opened doors to a variety of new nonfiction forms, not only reality programming but also confessional talk shows like *The Oprah Winfrey Show* (1986–present) and a wave of personal documentary films such as Ed Pincus's *Diaries* (1982) and Ross McElwee's *Sherman's March* (1986). Like Theodore Roszak's *The Making of a Counterculture*, *An American Family* asked audiences to think seriously about family, marital relations, sexuality, and affluence.[3] This realistic view of one family permanently demolished the "happy family" clichés of situation comedies of the 1950s and 1960s. Together with programs such as *The Mary Tyler Moore Show* (1970–77) and *All in the Family* (1971–79), *An American Family* transformed the representation of family life on American TV, introducing a new authenticity and diversity to fiction and nonfiction programs. In the intervening years, despite the hundreds of available channels and the vogue for "reality TV," American television has failed to produce creative nonfiction such as *An American Family*.

Acknowledgments

I would like to acknowledge the generosity of the people I interviewed during my research on *An American Family*: production secretary Alice Carey, National Educational Television president James Day, coordinating producer Jacqueline Donnet, assistant cameraman Tom Goodwin, series editor David Hanser, associate producer Susan Lester, cinematographer John Terry, and family member Lance Loud. Special thanks are due to producer Craig Gilbert, who answered endless queries about his experiences. Similarly, I am grateful to filmmakers Alan and Susan Raymond, who spent hours sharing their thoughts with me. In addition to their time and consideration, many of these producers lent me copies of their films and papers; Alan Raymond and Craig Gilbert provided most of the illustrations used in this book.

As a student at Cornell University, the University of Texas at Austin, Temple University, and the University of Iowa, I was blessed with outstanding professors who shared their time and ideas with me. At Cornell, David Grossvogel provided a shining example as a teacher and a scholar, and Glenn Altschuler offered general intellectual and moral support over many years. At UT-Austin, Jan Krawitz and William Stott nurtured my thinking about nonfiction film and photography. At Temple, Warren Bass, Richard Chalfen, Ben Levin, Jay Ruby, and Paul Swann encouraged my work in the history of documentary. Jay, in particular, shared his passion for visual anthropology and laid the groundwork for my research on *An American Family*. At the University of Iowa, Lauren Rabinovitz read innumerable drafts of this work and challenged me to explain my ideas more clearly. Richard Horwitz, Rick Altman, Dudley Andrew, and Franklin Miller also gave extensive advice on earlier versions.

Edward Branigan, Robert Burgoyne, Joanna Rapf, Carole Zucker, and Sarah Kozloff offered useful criticisms of my work on sound in documentary;

Steve Ungar, Albert Stone, and Wayne Franklin also commented on individual sections. Amy Petersen generously read and responded to a draft of the entire manuscript. A reader's report by Thomas Doherty of Brandeis University provided many detailed suggestions, which I have tried to incorporate into this final version. Jennifer Moore, my editor at the University of Minnesota Press, offered numerous ideas for improving this volume. My thanks to her and the Visible Evidence series editors—Michael Renov, Faye Ginsburg, and Jane Gaines—for their support. Helen Reiff made several valuable comments and deserves credit for indexing the book. I would also like to thank Alex Chapin for technical support. My parents and four brothers provided much encouragement during the long years of research and writing. Along the way, I had the pleasure of coauthoring a book about Japanese cinema and historical memory with my brother Kenneth. I am also grateful to my wife, Glennis Gold, and her parents for assistance with this project.

While working on the manuscript, I was invited to lecture on *An American Family* at New York University, Rice University, Ohio State University, Duke University, Kent University, and the University of North Carolina at Chapel Hill. To colleagues at these institutions, my thanks for their thoughtful responses. During 1993–94, while on a Fulbright grant in France, I presented segments of this work to scholars and students at the University of Iceland, the University of Helsinki, and the University of Amsterdam. I am beholden to Sigurjón Baldur Hafsteinsson, Seppo Tamminen, Thomas Elsaesser, and the Commission Franco-Américaine d'Echanges Universitaires et Culturels for these opportunities. Vassar, Middlebury, and Dartmouth Colleges contributed funds to illustrate this book, for which I am grateful.

A special thanks to Alan Raymond for frame enlargements from *An American Family* and to Craig Gilbert for the WNET publicity materials. Illustrations from *Empire, Gimme Shelter, High School, A Stravinsky Portrait,* and *Woodstock* appear courtesy of the Film Stills Archive, Museum of Modern Art. All other illustrations appear as credited in the captions.

Introduction
Recasting Documentary

An American Family was the most significant American documentary of
the 1970s and among the most influential television programs of that
decade. It reached an unusually broad audience for a nonfiction program;
Newsweek estimated ten million viewers for each episode, the high point
for public TV in the 1970s.[1] The size of the viewing public astonished the
program's production staff. "No one ever looked at public television," coordinating producer Jacqueline Donnet recalled. "We thought that we were
working on a little series like *The Working Musician.* Of course, there was
an audience out there, but we didn't think the family was going to make
the cover of *Newsweek.*" But the program had unusual resonance with
the general public. In the words of a *Chicago Tribune* reviewer, the documentary "made the trials of the Louds a shade better known than those of
Job. Everybody wrote about them and dissected them."[2] Journalist Merle
Miller, writing in *Esquire,* concurred, "I doubt if in the history of the tube
there has been so much talk about anything."[3] Cartoonists such as Garry
Trudeau and Jim Berry lampooned *An American Family.* To *not* watch the
show was an act of defiance. Novelist Elie Wiesel's refusal to join fellow
New Yorkers in front of a living room TV set was cited in the *New York
Times Magazine.* "One written sentence," Wiesel steadfastly maintained,
"is worth 800 hours of film."[4]

The first episode was broadcast by PBS on Thursday evening, January 11, 1973, at 9:00 P.M. (EST), at the same time as *Ironside* (1967–75)
on NBC, *The Thursday Night Movie* (John Frankenheimer's *The Gypsy
Moths,* 1969) on CBS, and an ABC premiere of Michelangelo Antonioni's
documentary *China* (1972). During its twelve-week run, *An American
Family* went against *Ironside* and *Kung Fu* (1972–75) and subsequent
movies on CBS, including Mark Robson's *Valley of the Dolls* (1967) and
Mike Nichols's *Who's Afraid of Virginia Woolf?* (1966). Despite the

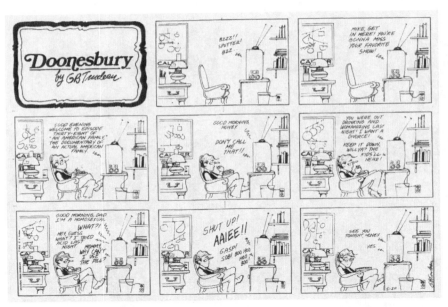

Doonesbury cartoon spoofs *An American Family. Doonesbury* copyright 1973
G. B. Trudeau. Reprinted with permission of Universal Press Syndicate; all rights
reserved.

competition on commercial networks, millions of viewers followed Pat and
Bill Loud's unfolding marital problems in a controversial show that some
critics called a real-life soap opera. As reviewer Stephanie Harrington
noted in the *New York Times,* "You find yourself sticking with the Louds
with the same compulsion that draws you back day after day to your
favorite soap opera."[5] People talked endlessly about the program, and the
Louds eventually received thousands of fan letters.[6]

The national press gave extensive coverage to the series in January,
February, March, and April 1973. Many critics panned it; others applauded. Divorce was a novel topic for prime time, and few viewers had ever encountered an openly gay son, such as Lance, on TV. Equally startling was
the style: an episodic documentary about family life with no expert commentary and no interviews. (By way of comparison, the 1973 Emmy Award
for cultural documentary went to a scripted historical series, *America,*
hosted by British émigré Alistair Cooke.) No less an authority than anthropologist Margaret Mead declared in an article in *TV Guide* that *An
American Family* was "as new and significant as the invention of drama
or the novel—a new way in which people can learn to look at life, by seeing
the real life of others interpreted by the camera."[7] As intended, Gilbert's
program provoked debates concerning family life and sexuality, the state
and character of the nation, and the role of television in American culture.

ARE YOU READY FOR "AN AMERICAN FAMILY"

There has never been anything on television—or anywhere else—to prepare you for "An American Family."

Producer Craig Gilbert has distilled seven crucial months in the lives of the William Loud family of California into 12 powerful full-hour films.

In doing so, he has captured the drama, humor and heartbreak of life—and given us an opportunity to understand, as never before, the forces affecting our families today.

"Nothing like it has ever been done," says Margaret Mead, "and I think it may be as important for our time as were the invention of drama and the novel."

The Louds are not actors. They had **?** no scripts. They simply lived. And were filmed.

During the filming, the family experienced profound upheaval, insight and change. Things so human, you may find yourself matching experiences with the Louds... comparing realities...gaining personal insight through the mirrors provided by these real people.

Next week Mrs. Loud visits her son in New York, and is confronted by his underground lifestyle. But before you can appreciate the events to come, you first have to meet the Louds.

Meet TV's first real family tonight. And share their lives in the 11 weeks to follow.

PREMIERE 9:00PM
CHANNEL 13
PBS PUBLIC BROADCASTING SERVICE

WNET-13's first ad for *An American Family*.

Reviews appeared not only in local, regional, and national newspapers, but in prestige publications such as *Harper's,* the *Atlantic, The Nation, Commentary, Society,* and *America.* Well-known cultural critics and intellectuals weighed in, including novelist Anne Roiphe, journalist Shana Alexander, linguist S. I. Hayakawa, novelist and critic Merle Miller, *New Yorker* editor Daniel Menaker, theater director Michael Murray, essayist Benjamin DeMott, author Abigail McCarthy, sociologist Herbert Gans, and many others. A number of these reviewers were highly critical of the Loud family. Alexander, author of *The Feminine Eye,* called the Louds "affluent zombies" in *Newsweek.*[8] Sociologist Irving Louis Horowitz, interviewed in *Time,* concluded that the family had "a tendency towards exhibitionism."[9] In an extended essay in the *New York Times Magazine,* feminist author Anne Roiphe struggled to come to terms with the gay son, Lance, calling him an "evil flower," an "electric eel," and a "Goyaesque emotional dwarf."[10] Many critics, like Roiphe, projected their fears about contemporary America onto the Louds.

Responding to criticisms of themselves and of the series, the Loud family and the producers vigorously entered this discussion, making *An American Family* the most hotly debated documentary ever broadcast on American television. The Louds gave interviews, wrote newspaper and magazine articles, and appeared on talk shows such as *The Phil Donahue Show* (1970–96) and *The Mike Douglas Show* (1961–82). By the time the family appeared on the March 12, 1973, cover of *Newsweek,* the seven members of this upper-middle-class family from Santa Barbara had become celebrities, attaining, in Andy Warhol's terms, their fifteen minutes of fame. "Eventually," one Harvard English professor noted in the *New Republic,* "we began to root for our favorite Loud."[11]

A media circus ensued. Rumors of an affair between producer Craig Gilbert and Pat Loud circulated, alluded to by Roiphe in the *New York Times Magazine* and then repeated by others in *Commonweal* and elsewhere.[12] As an antidote to the clichés of TV sitcoms, Gilbert tried to make a series about ordinary people and their everyday lives; he ended up making stars of the Louds. In February 1973, looking more and more like the Partridge Family, the five children performed as a rock band on *The Dick Cavett Show.* Lance, the charismatic son and erstwhile fan of Warhol, became a symbol for a generation of gay men discovering a more open lifestyle.[13] Offered an attractive contract by Coward, McCann & Geoghegan, Pat wrote her autobiography, *Pat Loud: A Woman's Story,* taking up the mantle of the liberated housewife on a nationwide book tour. Bill, for his part, was solicited to host a television game show.[14] Media appearances

MILLIONS WATCHED HER MARRIAGE
FALL APART—NOW PAT LOUD HAS WRITTEN
A FRANK AND DEVASTATING BOOK
ABOUT HERSELF, HER FAMILY AND THE TV
SERIES THAT FASCINATED AMERICA.

PAT LOUD
A WOMAN'S STORY
PAT LOUD WITH NORA JOHNSON

Pat Loud on the cover of her autobiography, published in 1974. Published by Bantam Dell Publishing Group; used by permission of Bantam Dell Publishing Group, a division of Random House, Inc.

multiplied: Delilah went on to appear as a "bachelorette" on *The Dating Game*, and Lance posed in the nude for *Screw* magazine. Although the series was widely viewed when first broadcast, and it turned the Louds into celebrities, *An American Family* has received little attention since 1973. In *Prime-Time Families*, a study of the representation of family life on television in the 1970s, TV scholar Ella Taylor makes no mention of the series.[15]

▶

From Conception to Reception

In this volume, I examine the controversial documentary *An American Family* from conception to reception. Most analyses of films and television shows proceed from the assumption that the finished work alone deserves study. But to view a program as a fait accompli is to fail to recognize how it could have been different. Film theorist Rick Altman makes this point in his introduction to *Sound Theory/Sound Practice:* "If we consider for a moment the lengthy process of conception-investment-production-distribution-exhibition-reception, we recognize that the completed film constitutes the only step in the procession representing apparent unity."[16] This book charts "the lengthy process" of the making and broadcast of *An American Family.*

The twelve-episode observational documentary was an experiment in nonfiction media, an exceptional program that broke the rules of television production. Under Gilbert's supervision, filmmakers Susan Raymond and Alan Raymond recorded the everyday lives of the Louds from May 30 through December 31, 1971. The extensive filming gave the crew and family ample time to get to know one another, so that the family members could live in the presence of a camera crew and the filmmakers could become temporary members of the family. More than three hundred hours of 16mm color film were shot. The editing process took more than a year and involved a team of people working at National Educational Television (NET) in New York City.

Many of *An American Family*'s innovations—the use of lightweight portable cameras and wireless microphones, the recording of spontaneous action without scripts, the telling of a nonfiction narrative in episodic, serial form—were later absorbed into commercial television in modified forms. In chapter 1, I focus on the institutional framework of public television in the early 1970s, producer Craig Gilbert's original intentions, and the work of a talented group of professionals at NET. Why did the Corporation for Public Broadcasting and the Ford Foundation provide $1.2 million to make such an unorthodox series? From the many families in the United States at the time, how and why did Gilbert select the Louds?

Alan and Susan Raymond film the Loud family at dinner.

Chapter 2 follows the production process through shooting and editing. On an average day, Susan Raymond, sound recordist, and Alan Raymond, cinematographer, were on location from late morning until evening. In keeping with the observational style, they tried to downplay their own actions. "We really believed rigidly in 'fly on the wall' observation," Susan later recalled. "It's a very Zen exercise to try to diminish your presence as best you can. We were totally dedicated to that for every single day of the shooting." But when the camera was not rolling, personal friendships gradually formed between the Raymonds and the Louds. When the filming ended, Pat was sorry to see them go.[17] Once the footage had been shot, Gilbert and the editors pieced together twelve hour-long episodes, a mere fraction of the seven months spent with the family. What principles of selection were followed? What scenes were left out?

Filmmaking is a collaborative process, one not without conflict. With this in mind, I try to give equal attention here to the work of the producer, the cinematographer and sound recordist, the associate and coordinating producers, and the editors. Over a period of years, I interviewed most of the individuals involved in the making of *An American Family*. Whenever possible, they tell this story in their own words. (All quotations in the text for which sources are not provided in notes come from these interviews.) The production study reasserts the importance of producers, their intentions, and the institutions that support, and constrain, their work. If producers themselves had no role in the production of

Delilah, 15, (left) and her sister Michele, 13, members of the William C. Loud family of Santa Barbara, California. Together with their parents and three brothers, the girls are the subjects of AN AMERICAN FAMILY, WNET/13's landmark series of 12 hour-long documentaries. Producer Craig Gilbert and his camera crews spent seven months living with the Louds, recording their day-to-day lives. AN AMERICAN FAMILY, a unique panorama of contemporary American life, premieres in New York on WNET/13 and nationally over the Public Broadcasting Service on Thursday, January 11 at 9:00 p.m. (Please check your local PBS station for area broadcast time.)

Delilah and Michele Loud in a WNET publicity photograph.

meaning, there would be little meaningful incentive to make films and television programs.

In the *International Dictionary of Films and Filmmakers,* film scholar Robin Wood calls Jean Renoir's *Rules of the Game* (1939) one of the cinema's "truly inexhaustible" works.[18] The same may be said of *An American Family,* although for somewhat different reasons. The richness of Gilbert's twelve-hour documentary lies somewhere between that of Renoir's masterpiece and, for example, the many decades of televised episodes of *The Guiding Light* (1952–present). Chapters 3, 4, and 5 place *An American Family* within the evolving history of film and television style. The images and sounds of the series are central here. Although known widely as an example of observational cinema, the program mixes the narrative traditions of the media industries, marrying the innovations of American observational cinema to the narrative traditions of TV. Whereas most nonfiction programming, particularly television news, speaks directly to the audience, Gilbert's program, like other observational films, addresses the viewer obliquely through the telling of a story. Although common in the independent film community by the 1970s, this observational style had never found such a large TV audience.

An American Family uses an episodic, multiple-focus structure common to soap operas. Like daytime television serials, it postpones closure in favor of process, emphasizes intimate daily life, focuses on multiple characters over plot, and presents a melodramatic cosmos. Although serial structure had been used on American television for many years, it was unusual for documentary at the time. The first show introduces the seven Louds and the central story line, and the next eleven programs follow their activities in the summer and fall of 1971. Episode one gives away the drama of the series—the parents' eventual separation—immediately, so that viewers are primed to read all subsequent events as telltale signs of the decline of Pat and Bill's marriage. With this crucial exception, the series proceeds in a loose chronological order. Individual shows emphasize certain characters over others; hour seven, for example, explores Grant's attitude toward his summer job. Each subsequent episode builds upon the developments showcased in earlier ones, as when Pat, in episode nine, asks Bill for a divorce, following through on the dissatisfaction she expressed in the previous show.

Although there are multiple stories in *An American Family,* the dominant plotline involves the marital problems of Mr. and Mrs. Loud. Other developments explored include the relations between the Louds and their children; the affairs of Bill's company, American Western Foundries; Lance's activities in New York City and his travels in Europe; Delilah's dance rehearsals and performance as well as her budding relationship with boyfriend Brad (one of the underdeveloped stories); Pat's visit to her mother in Eugene, Oregon, and her vacation in Taos, New Mexico; Kevin's business trip to Southeast Asia (another story line more absent than present); Grant's summer job as a construction worker; and the evolution of the boys' garage band. Throughout, the documentary rarely veers from immediate concerns with interpersonal relationships. Of a filmed discussion between Bill Loud and striking longshoremen in San Francisco about the Vietnam War, coordinating producer Donnet said, "You could have made an hour show on that discussion alone. But there was just no way to fit it in. It didn't move forward the story of the family."

An American Family is not entirely unified or consistent. In numerous instances, Gilbert circumvents the emphasis on a strictly observational style. A distinctly hybrid work, the documentary represents, in the words of Yale drama professor Richard Gilman, a "bastard union of several forms."[19] Brief uses of an on-camera host, voice-over narration, scored music, and home movies show the director's commitment to other modes of nonfiction address. Furthermore, the twelve-part documentary struggles against its own formative, and interpretive, tendencies, striving to show "life as it is" while simultaneously criticizing American society in the early

Delilah Loud and her boyfriend, Brad, in *An American Family.*

1970s. Like the Loud family it depicts, *An American Family* is a text at war with itself. Although it might be possible to write film and television history without examining the works themselves, this volume reaffirms the capital, if no longer central, role of close analysis in media studies.

As one of the most popular, and controversial, documentaries ever made, *An American Family* offers an excellent case study of audience reactions. In chapters 6 and 7, by considering the variety of responses, I bring out the interpretive role of publicists, critics, and viewers. Even before audience members tuned in, the publicity campaign laid out terms that reviewers could borrow to characterize the series. Publicity set the stage for published responses, especially as the WNET press releases were more didactic than the documentary itself. Although frequently ignored by audience studies, press materials and advertisements supply important frames of reference.

Many critics failed to recognize the mediation involved in *An American Family* and talked about the Louds as if they were their next-door neighbors. These newspaper and magazine reviewers analyzed the family rather than the documentary. On the other hand, some writers recognized the show as a rhetorical construct and identified themes; the dominant interpretation was that the program chronicled the breakdown of American culture. Others tried to find generic comparisons, but the hybrid nature of the series defied easy definition. As Margaret Mead noted in *TV Guide,* "I do not think *An American Family* should be called a documentary. I think we need a new name for it, a name that would contrast it not only with fiction, but with what we have been exposed to up until now on TV."[20] Still others rejected out of hand the basic premises of observational cinema and used the series as an opportunity to criticize the medium of television itself, which they felt was creating a society of spectacle. Shocked and confused, the Louds themselves tried to influence the public response by disputing criticisms of their lives and by calling attention to the editing of the program. Their subsequent appearances on talk shows gradually turned *An American Family* into a media event.

In chapter 8, I explore the enduring impact of the series on representations of family life in American film and television and offer a postscript on the subsequent careers of the producers and the Louds. True to its hybrid form, *An American Family* influenced the evolution not only of nonfiction film and TV, but of fictional series, including *One Day at a Time* (1975–84), *Family* (1976–80), and *A Year in the Life* (1987–88) as well as feature films such as *An Unmarried Woman* (Paul Mazursky, 1978) and *Ordinary People* (Robert Redford, 1980).

This volume presents a comprehensive portrait of *An American Family*. The production history provides essential information about its making, details one could never know simply from watching the series. The stylistic analysis shows how carefully crafted the documentary was, how image, sound, and editing were employed to construct a plausible image of everyday life and an argument about contemporary society. The reception study indicates the wide variety of conflicting responses the series actually generated. Although it remains fashionable to celebrate the role of viewers, and by extension of reviewers, in the making of meaning, as often as not reactions to *An American Family* were silly, based on superficial impressions and unexamined assumptions. In this book, I argue for a holistic approach to films and television shows. I follow the process of making meaning along a daisy chain of signification, detailing the roles of public television institutions, producers, filmmakers, subjects, reviewers, and audience members in the production and reception of *An American Family*.[21]

I Making *An American Family*

[1] "A Real View of Middle-Class Life"

Real life depiction is not the same as real life.
:: Craig Gilbert[1]

An American Family did not emerge out of a vacuum; rather, it represents
the culmination of a decade of documentary expression and independent
cinema and is strongly tied to other currents in the arts. Craig Gilbert ma-
tured as a maker of documentaries during the 1960s, an exciting period for
filmmaking in New York City, with a burgeoning independent production
community whose evolution coincided with the growth of public broadcasting. The civil rights movement, the antiwar movement, and emerging
countercultures spawned a new journalism and gave many documentarists
a sense of urgency about their work. Film production costs fell, and funds
became available from the new National Endowment for the Humanities
and the National Endowment for the Arts, as well as the new state arts
councils. NET, the forerunner of the public broadcasting system, became
the primary source of programming for educational TV stations throughout the United States.

Although he spent his entire professional career in television, Gilbert
was aware of the work of the independent documentary filmmakers. An
observational style developed within this community in the late 1950s and
1960s, taking advantage of new lightweight portable cameras and tape
recorders. Gilbert saw the groundbreaking films of Drew Associates, *Primary* (1960) and *The Chair* (1963); Richard Leacock's *A Happy Mother's
Day* (1963), *A Stravinsky Portrait* (1965), and *Chiefs* (1968); D. A. Pennebaker's *Don't Look Back* (1967); Albert and David Maysles's *Salesman*
(1969) and *Gimme Shelter* (1970); and Frederick Wiseman's institutional
documentaries of the late 1960s.[2] Many of these works explored social issues through a less didactic style that had as much in common with fiction

Igor Stravinsky in Richard Leacock's *A Stravinsky Portrait*.

as with the documentary tradition. (Some film historians refer to observational cinema as cinema verité or direct cinema. I discuss the development and evolution of this style of cinema in detail in chapter 3.) Gilbert drew on these documentaries for the style of *An American Family*.

Like other producers, Gilbert followed the work of the new nonfiction journalists who were publishing in the *New Yorker,* the *Atlantic, New York,* and other magazines. He described himself as an "enormous fan" of novelists Truman Capote, Tom Wolfe, Joan Didion, Norman Mailer, and others who adapted narrative techniques to literary nonfiction. New journalists used a wide variety of styles, including first-person narration, confessional tales, humor, and irony. Works such as Capote's *In Cold Blood* (1965), Wolfe's *The Electric Kool-Aid Acid Test* (1966), Didion's *Slouching Towards Bethlehem* (1968), and Mailer's *Armies of the Night* (1968) opened up new possibilities for documentary producers. The Maysles brothers, in particular, saw their films as counterparts to the nonfiction novel. In 1966, they completed *With Love from Truman: A Visit with Truman Capote*, produced by National Educational Television. Through Wolfe, Gilbert met Ken Kesey, author of *One Flew over the Cuckoo's Nest* (1962), and had an opportunity to make a film about Kesey's celebrated 1967 cross-country bus trip, one of many NET proposals that was never funded.

NET and Producer Craig Gilbert

To understand *An American Family* is, in part, to understand the history of public broadcasting, for the series was produced by NET, at a cost of $1.2 million, and distributed by the new Public Broadcasting Service to member stations in 1973. *An American Family* would never have been produced by the commercial networks ABC, NBC, or CBS, which, by the early 1970s, had scaled back documentary production, in the race for audience ratings.[3] Unlike the commercial networks in the 1970s, public television was not driven to seek the largest possible audience of potential consumers for advertisers. As a result, producers could explore innovative styles and subject matter. Some critics, including James Day, former president of NET, doubt that an innovative series such as *An American Family* could have been made *at any other time* in the history of public TV, given the administrative structure of PBS and the turn to corporate underwriting for individual programs after President Richard Nixon vetoed the 1972 Corporation for Public Broadcasting budget. After 1973, staff producers at member stations were bound, through ties to corporate funding, to conventional styles and non-controversial subject matter.

In 1963, with the support of the Ford Foundation, National Educational Television was created with a mandate to produce five hours per week of programming, primarily in the areas of cultural and public affairs. From 1963 to 1970, the Ford Foundation provided NET with approximately eight million dollars a year, promoting high-quality works on educational TV.[4] As a result, NET was not obliged to seek additional support, which gave its producers a degree of autonomy; initial lump-sum payments were less constraining than later piecemeal grants from corporations. In 1971, NET obtained six hundred thousand dollars from the Ford Foundation for the production of *An American Family*, with the Corporation for Public Broadcasting providing an additional six hundred thousand.

The late 1960s and early 1970s were tumultuous times for public television. In 1969, CPB, together with the Ford Foundation and representatives of regional stations, created PBS to serve as a national interconnection system. With the creation of CPB and PBS, and with a commitment of federal support after years of lobbying, the Ford Foundation reduced its involvement in public TV. NET merged in June 1970 with the local New York station WNDT-13 to become WNET-13, one of the flagship stations in the new PBS consortium. NET president James Day became the interim president of WNET-13 and fired the main personnel from NET, whose positions went to WNDT staff.

It was during this interim period in the history of educational TV, 1970–73, that *An American Family* was made. In these changing circumstances, Craig Gilbert managed to obtain support for an unconventional twelve-episode documentary. By the time the program was broadcast, NET had ceased to exist; even James Day had departed. According to Day, "*An American Family* was the only series that really suffered from the change-over from NET to Channel 13." The turnover in personnel had important ramifications, because the new WNET administrators had little allegiance to a program initiated by their predecessors. Suddenly, producer Gilbert was left on his own to fend for his ambitious series.

■───

Gilbert's Background

The making of *An American Family* supports the notion that television is a "producer's medium." Although Craig Gilbert did not perform any technical role on the series, he supervised all the creative and logistical stages of production, from conception to broadcast. His formation within the TV industry was the most decisive factor in his professional worldview, a training that distinguishes him from other major documentary auteurs of his generation, such as Drew, Leacock, Pennebaker, and Wiseman. These filmmakers all became independent producers. Gilbert was never part of the "Drew-Leacock old-boy network," as he called it. "These are people who considered themselves the elder statesmen of cinema verité. They lived, breathed, and ate film. I didn't and I haven't ever." Documentary film historians—favoring film over television, directors over producers, authorial consistency over eclecticism, and critical successes over popular ones—have consequently neglected Gilbert's work.[5]

Born in 1926, Gilbert grew up in an upper-middle-class family in Woodmere, Long Island. His father was a copyright lawyer at Schirmer Music; his mother worked in the home. He attended Andover, a private prep school, and then Harvard College, where he majored in English literature. After graduating from college, he hoped to be a writer. "I started out thinking I was going to write the great American novel," Gilbert recalled, "and I made a rather feeble stab at that." In the fall of 1950, he found work as a production assistant on instructional documentaries for the U.S. Navy. In 1951, he apprenticed as an editor for *The March of Time* (1935–51), a weekly newsreel that combined actuality footage and reenactments. Later, he worked on NBC's *Victory at Sea* (1952–53), a twenty-six-episode compilation series on naval warfare during World War II, a critical and popular success. Although he realized that he was not

Craig Gilbert, producer of AN AMERICAN FAMILY, WNET/13's landmark series of 12 hour-long documentaries. Gilbert, who conceived the series, and his camera crews spent seven months living with the William C. Loud family of Santa Barbara, California, recording their day-to-day lives. AN AMERICAN FAMILY, a unique panorama of contemporary American life, premieres in New York on WNET/13 and nationally over the Public Broadcasting Service on Thursday, January 11 at 9:00 p.m. (Please check your local PBS station for area broadcast time.)

Craig Gilbert in a WNET publicity photograph.

destined to be a film editor, by this time he had become fascinated with nonfiction production.

On the advice of a producer at CBS, Gilbert took a job with Fairchild Publications, publisher of *Women's Wear Daily*. After a year of print journalism, he worked as a writer, editor, and researcher on the third pilot of CBS's *Lowell Thomas Remembers* (1954), another archival series. Following a brief stint at NBC, he was offered a job by the head of public affairs at CBS to work on a Sunday-morning travelogue show for children hosted by Sonny Fox. From 1955 to 1957, Gilbert honed his skills as a writer on *Let's Take a Trip* (1955–58). "It's not Norman Mailer. It is not playwriting. It is not screenwriting. It's a peculiar kind of television writing." He had a knack for this kind of work, which required a concise vocabulary and a precise sense of timing. In essayist Ved Mehta's words, "The discipline of television writing is a bit like that of writing haiku, but with little poetry."[6] From 1957 to 1960, Gilbert also freelanced on network programs that showcased the outstanding baseball and football games of the week.

In 1960, Gilbert directed his first TV show, a CBS documentary on football, *Seven Days to Kick Off*, shot at the U.S. Air Force Academy. In the ensuing three years, although he was not particularly interested in fiction, he wrote short plays that were broadcast on Sunday mornings; one dealt with racial intolerance. In 1963, he continued his work as a director on the cultural affairs series *Chronicle*, a sixty-minute magazine show, making portraits of artists such as sculptor Jacques Lipschitz, painter Pablo Picasso, and novelist Wallace Stegner. In 1964, he left CBS to work at NET.

National Educational Television was a small organization when Craig Gilbert joined the ranks as a producer in the mid-1960s; it was run primarily by John White, president; William Kobin, head of programming; Don Dixon, head of public affairs programming; and Don Kellerman, head of cultural affairs. Gilbert was hired by Kellerman to produce a weekly program, *Magazine of the Arts*, and, intrigued by the politics of the counterculture, he did a show about folksingers Buffy Sainte-Marie, Tom Paxton, and Phil Ochs. He later produced and directed a program about sculptors George Segal and John Chamberlain. *Magazine of the Arts* was discontinued when Kellerman was fired and White discovered that Gilbert had been taken on without authorization.

Curtis Davis became the new head of cultural affairs at NET. The programs Gilbert had produced were incorporated into a new series, *The Creative Person*. For the new show, Gilbert did portraits of the poet William Carlos Williams, industrial designer Raymond Loewy, entertainers Ossie Davis and Ruby Dee, and opera impresario Rudolf Bing. Like much of the cultural programming at NET in the 1960s, his work focused primarily on bringing traditional fine arts subjects to TV. Gilbert's career in documentary spans the old *March of Time* tradition as well as the new forms that emerged in the 1960s. He became adept at making shows on demand on a wide variety of topics. Unlike other documentary filmmakers, such as Leacock, Pennebaker, and Wiseman, Gilbert received his training almost entirely within the television industry.

Although Gilbert produced many kinds of programs for commercial and public television, he aspired to make feature-length works. When the Carnegie Commission published its report on educational television in 1967, administrators at NET recognized plans to transform public TV radically. In response, the head of programming initiated a policy of producing "blockbusters," high-profile shows to call attention to the work of NET. As a staff producer, Gilbert was required to submit ideas for ambitious programs. Having read of Margaret Mead's plans to return to the island where she had first done fieldwork, he proposed to do a film about her trip. To his astonishment, this proposal was accepted by *NET Journal* (1966–70) and Gilbert met the famous anthropologist, who would become his close friend.

The most celebrated anthropologist in the United States since the 1928 publication of her book *Coming of Age in Samoa,* Mead had a reputation as a spokeswoman for progressive social ideas. She had long championed film and photography in anthropological research, making some of the first, and still some of the most thorough, uses of visual media in the field. As such, Mead represented a pivotal figure for a nonfiction film portrait, and the resulting work sheds some light on Gilbert's methods. "She put me through a whole series of tests," he recalled. "She was an incredible pain in the ass." Prior to her return to New Guinea, Mead insisted that the producer hire a crew to film her at a conference in Greece. The resulting footage was useless for the producer's purposes, but it persuaded Mead to go ahead with the project.

Gilbert did no technical work on this feature documentary or on any of his later works. Like a Hollywood director, he preferred "to see the overall picture without being encumbered with a camera or a tape recorder." Richard Leiterman, the talented cinematographer who would later shoot Wiseman's *High School* (1969) and Allan King's *A Married Couple* (1969), filmed *Margaret Mead's New Guinea Journal.* The shoot was complicated by the crew's inability to screen the rushes on location. Upon his return to Manhattan, Gilbert discovered that the exposed, unprocessed, film stock was languishing on a shelf at NET because the center had run out of money. He struggled to find outside funding, and eventually his family contributed money to finish the film.

On December 3, 1968, NET broadcast the first feature-length documentary by Craig Gilbert, *Margaret Mead's New Guinea Journal.* (Actually,

Richard Leiterman, cinematographer of *A Married Couple*. Courtesy of Allan King Associates, Ltd.

in the absence of a satellite hookup, the program was duplicated numerous times at facilities in Ann Arbor, Michigan, and mailed to stations across the country.) Extensive archival photographs, newsreel footage, and contemporary scenes, together with first-person and third-person voice-over narration, told the story of the island and Mead's work there from the colonial period through independence. Mead appeared as a village elder, and the film touched on standard ceremonies of interest to anthropologists: birth, death, religious activities, and civic affairs. The documentary is still an important portrait of Mead, a pivotal and controversial figure in anthropology.

The Triumph of Christy Brown

In 1969, when Gilbert got funding to make a feature documentary about the Irish novelist Christy Brown, Richard Leiterman was not available to shoot it. "One of the problems with working at NET was that there was no continuity of money," Gilbert recalled. "It was very difficult to have a continuity of crew. In other words, if you found a cameraman that you liked, you could not have this man under contract. You could not be sure that you would have him for future projects." Fern McBride, a producer at NET, suggested a young cinematographer named Alan Raymond, who had just shot *Glen and Randa* (1971), an independent fiction film directed by McBride's husband, Jim.

A generation younger than Craig Gilbert, Raymond was a proponent of the new observational documentary style. He grew up in New York and graduated from a public high school in Queens. His father was a college professor. Raymond attended New York University in the early 1960s, majoring in filmmaking at the same time as Jim McBride, Martin Scorsese, and Michael Wadleigh, who all later distinguished themselves in documentary as well as fiction film. Raymond synchronized rushes for Drew Associates while still in school. Fresh out of college, he edited for William Jersey, whose documentary on racial integration in Nebraska, *A Time for Burning,* was well received in 1967. Alan's fiancée, Susan Cullinan (later Raymond), also worked for Jersey. She grew up in Broadview, Illinois, and, inspired by Margaret Mead, majored in sociology at DePaul University. Shortly after they were married, the Raymonds started working as a two-person crew for the Maysles brothers, with Alan doing camera and Susan recording sound.

Gilbert hired the Raymonds to film in Ireland. To his delight, the shoot went well, and they made plans to work together on future projects. From *The Triumph of Christy Brown,* it is clear that Gilbert, unlike Wiseman, is stylistically eclectic, willing to borrow techniques from the entire documentary tradition to tell an engaging story, including voice-over narration, archival photographs and newsreel footage, interviews, observational scenes, scored music, and even reenactments based on events from Brown's autobiographical novel *Down All the Days* (1970). On October 12, 1970, NET broadcast *The Triumph of Christy Brown,* which told the moving story of a man who overcame physical disability to become a talented writer. (In 1989, Brown was the subject of the Academy Award–winning biopic *My Left Foot,* directed by Jim Sheridan and based in part on Gilbert's documentary.) Whereas *Margaret Mead's New Guinea Journal* represented a personal success for Gilbert, *The Triumph of Christy Brown* won an Emmy Award and was praised by critics around the country.

■──

"A Real View of Middle-Class Life"

In early 1971, however, Craig Gilbert was depressed. Despite his having won an Emmy, his job as staff producer at NET was in jeopardy due to the institutional changes in public television. Furthermore, his private life was in shambles. Like many of his friends in Greenwich Village, he found himself divorced after years of marriage.[7] Alan Raymond described his state of mind: "Craig's view of life is a pessimistic one. He's the kind of person who reads those books called *Surviving the Seventies, What Does It All Really Mean?* and *Where Are We Now That the Bomb Hangs Over Us All?*"[8] Gilbert's personal life seemed to mirror the increasingly polarized state of the nation after 1968. But at a time when other producers were making controversial social-issue documentaries, such as Peter Davis's *Hunger in America* (1967), Felix Greene's *Inside North Vietnam* (1968), and Mort Silverstein's *Banks and the Poor* (1970), he had made portraits of personalities in the arts.

Like Gilbert, NET president James Day believed that NET needed to address the vast changes that were occurring in American society, "particularly with young people—their attitudes towards drugs, towards sex, towards religion." The Public Affairs Department promised a new series of provocative investigative reports of these issues, *Priorities for Change.* According to Susan Lester, associate producer of *An American Family*: "One would have been about drugs. One would have been about the generation gap. I'm sure one would have been about divorce. One would have been about all of these things that were dividing up this country so radically. They would have been rather conventional presentations of material. These kinds of documentaries are still done today."

Prepared to look for another job, Gilbert asked to be laid off from NET so that he could receive unemployment compensation. Before honoring his request, however, Curtis Davis, a strong supporter of Gilbert's work, asked him to draw up a proposal for another blockbuster. "Over the weekend," Gilbert recalled, "I was to write an outline of the TV program I most wanted to do. I was to pay no attention to the normal restrictions of time, money, or practicality."[9] Inspired by Allan King's documentary *A Married Couple,* the producer decided he wanted to make a film about family in contemporary America. Using an observational style, *A Married Couple* portrayed ten weeks in what director King called a "marriage in crisis."[10] Gilbert dismissed standard approaches to this subject matter, such as traveling "around the country interviewing people—all ages of married and unmarried women, all ages of married and unmarried men, therapists, marriage counselors, religious figures, anthropologists, sociologists, and so on."[11] Following King's example, Gilbert suggested making a nonfiction TV series, without any script, based on whatever happened in the life of one family over the course of a year. The proposal represented a radical rejection of typical production methods. In television, as in Hollywood cinema, the script represents the cornerstone of editorial control and censorship; directors are not allowed to make films without scripts.

Like many social critics of the period, Gilbert believed that the Ameri-

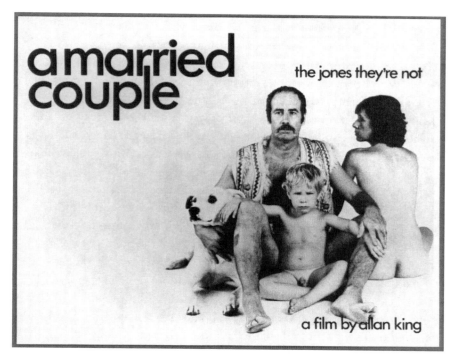

A publicity still for Allan King's *A Married Couple*. Courtesy of Allan King
Associates, Ltd.

can family was disappearing, becoming "obsolete."[12] Indeed, the family had
become the central arena for debates about the state of American culture,
epitomized in works like Theodore Roszak's *The Making of a Counterculture* and Charles Reich's *The Greening of America,* critiques with which
Gilbert was familiar.[13] In the 1970s, social theorists had come to think of
the family as "an intimate battleground."[14] Arguments about the state of
American society pivoted around particular visions of family life, fueled by
anxiety over the divorce rate, the women's movement, new sexual mores,
gay liberation, and the generation gap. Reich's radical critique of American
society included the role of the media: "Many attitudes, points of view,
and pictures of reality cannot get shown on television; this includes not
only political ideas, but also the strictly non-political, such as a real view
of middle-class life in place of the cheerful comedies one usually sees."[15]
Reich's analysis of contemporary malaise offered a blueprint for Gilbert's
series. *An American Family* was Gilbert's attempt to put "a real view of
middle-class life" on prime-time television.

Craig Gilbert was not the only producer who reacted against idealized
images of American family life presented on TV. Others, such as Norman
Lear, whose company made *All in the Family* (1971–79), also transformed

the depiction of families on television in the 1970s. Producers James L. Brooks and Allan Burns tried to make the main character on *The Mary Tyler Moore Show* (1970–77) a divorcée, but the networks refused to allow it.[16] Cinematographer Alan Raymond later summarized the guiding premise behind Gilbert's attempt to provide an alternative perspective to happy situation comedies: "An entire generation of viewers was unconsciously traumatized because they could never measure up to the image of family life they saw on the screen."[17] For the producers of *An American Family,* television was as much of a problem in American society as actual family life.

Shortly before Gilbert proposed his idea for the series, *Time* magazine ran an article titled "The American Family—Future Uncertain" in its December 28, 1970, issue. Gilbert's intuition about marriage and family was not without foundation: "Between 1965 and 1975 the number of divorces granted each year in the United States more than doubled."[18] The producer believed that one family's experiences would capture life in general in the early 1970s, because, in his opinion, all Americans, of different classes, religions, and ethnic groups, share certain myths, beliefs, and values; all are subjected to the tensions and characteristics of the age.[19] Although Gilbert was proud of his earlier documentaries, he thought that television viewers would identify more readily with the daily problems of an ordinary family than with the lives of celebrities such as Christy Brown and Margaret Mead. Not surprisingly, the producer's interest in the study of everyday life had grown during his work with the renowned anthropologist. Mead herself was a steadfast advocate of Gilbert's idea. Curtis Davis, who was also dissatisfied with conventional social-issue documentaries, wholeheartedly supported Gilbert's proposal.

The head of cultural affairs and the producer pitched the idea to James Day. The NET president saw the virtues of such an unusual nonfiction series about contemporary American life. He later acknowledged, "The notion of treating the issue of changing values in a more dramatic, less didactic, less ordinary context than the conventional documentary form was more than tempting, it was irresistible."[20] Having put together his dream proposal, Gilbert was astonished when Day committed the organization to the production of *An American Family.* On short notice, the funds for *Priorities for Change* were switched over in their entirety to Gilbert's nonfiction program. The scale and ambition of the show promised to put PBS, a new entity, on the map of cultural programming in the United States.

It was no accident that Gilbert's project received funding; it was a programming coup in a shifting, uncertain situation. Whereas his first two documentaries merely extended his earlier portraits to feature length, *An American Family* represented a quantum leap forward in nonfiction subject matter and style. Following Charles Reich's call for a radical TV, Gilbert wanted to make a series about the politics of everyday life, subverting public television's timidity in cultural programs. In *Television: The Business behind the Box,* TV critic Les Brown details PBS's structural fear of controversy: "The trick to running most public TV stations successfully is not to serve the public in the fullest but to serve the local board of directors, and in a majority of situations that is accomplished through an avoidance of controversy."[21] Although PBS abhors controversial programming, no show did more to call attention to the fledgling network than *An American Family.*

▶ ──

Finding a Family

> *We were not looking for a typical family. We were looking for a family that sells Cracker Jacks. The kind of family that you see on a television commercial, in a pretty house, that has the best of what this country can offer materially.*
> :: Susan Lester, associate producer

Most producers, laboring under difficult constraints, prefer to remain within established genres, which simplifies the production process. News organizations control the unpredictability of the real world by standardizing techniques for reporting and packaging current events. Craig Gilbert opened all of this up by admitting that accepted practices for representing reality were arbitrary. Working without a script, Gilbert tried to reinvent the rules of television production. But new methods create problems. Because observational cinema generally thrives on spontaneity and chance, forms and practices must be improvised in the process.

According to Gilbert, "The essential talent involved in the making of a documentary, particularly in the making of cinema verité films, is the picking of the subject." Simply on the basis of the location, in his view, Wiseman was guaranteed dramatic footage for *Hospital* (1970). Filming in the emergency ward at the Metropolitan Hospital Center in Manhattan was, in Gilbert's words, "like shooting fish in a barrel." Many documentary filmmakers feel, conversely, that the essential talent in observational cinema lies in the skill and intelligence of the cinematographer, the sound recordist, and, to a lesser extent, the editor. Like Richard Leacock, Alan Raymond maintains that the cinematographer counts the most. As a producer, however, Gilbert saw technical personnel as relatively interchangeable.

Gilbert spent months looking for a family for his series. Nonfiction

A scene from Frederick Wiseman's *Hospital*. Courtesy of Zipporah Films.

filmmakers rarely talk about this aspect of their work, which amounts to
the documentary equivalent of casting. Paul Wilkes, the associate producer
of *Six American Families* (1976), a PBS series inspired by *An American
Family*, outlined the casting for an episode shot in Chicago. He set out to
find "the family of a blue-collar worker with children still at home, with a
living relative who had emigrated from Poland; a family whose Polishness
is dear to them."[22] Similarly, director Connie Field described this process
for her independent documentary *The Life and Times of Rosie the Riveter*
(1980): "We did extensive preinterviews—seven hundred women were
interviewed over the phone, two hundred in person on audio tape, thirty-
five were videotaped; and we filmed five."[23] The choice of subjects for
nonfiction programs is not haphazard; people typically appear in documentaries because they meet the requirements of the producers.

Having received the go-ahead from the president of NET, Gilbert was
urged by friends to select an African American family. The producer had
the freedom to consider whatever family he wanted. There were, at least
theoretically, more than fifty million American families available in 1971.
The few dozen Gilbert interviewed all agreed to take part. Although he was
tempted to select a black family, he eventually chose an upper-middle-class
Euro-American one. Not surprisingly, Gilbert had a particular kind of fami-

ly in mind for *An American Family.* Like any good documentary producer, he knew what he was seeking. He had ideas that he wanted to express about life in the United States. As it happened, Gilbert was more interested in representations of class and gender than in issues of racial and ethnic identity.

From the outset, the producer envisioned a family that would look reasonably like those featured on television situation comedies throughout the 1950s and 1960s, such as *Father Knows Best* (1954–60) and *The Donna Reed Show* (1958–66). "In all these shows," Gilbert later wrote, "the family was middle-class, attractive, and lived in a house (as opposed to an apartment) in what appeared to be a suburb of a large city."[24] Gilbert believed that these fictional programs presented an ideal lifestyle to which viewers aspired, a mass-mediated version of the American dream.

Like Wiseman, who chose a middle-class high school—one that community members would generally regard as successful—for *High School,* Gilbert wanted a family that seemingly had it all. Susan Lester echoed this point of view: "One of the early decisions was not to have a family that a viewer would look at and say, 'If only they weren't black and underprivileged. If only they didn't live in Watts. If only this kid could get a scholarship to school. If only the father could get a job.' Material success was important in what we were trying to say because we were trying to play around with the American dream." Like another documentary of the period, *But What If the Dream Comes True?* (Markowitz, CBS, 1972), *An American Family* would examine what happened when a family obtained the trappings of the good life.

Gilbert limited his search to California because he believed that the West Coast represented the cutting edge of American culture, that issues and trends were flowing east from the country's most populous state. Indeed, in 1970, California passed a law that enabled couples to divorce without bringing charges against one another, an important precedent.[25] Adopting Frederick Jackson Turner's frontier thesis, the producer thought that California offered the last frontier, a place where Americans were drawn to pursue their dreams, unfettered by history and tradition. Accordingly, the ideal family would be first-generation immigrants to the state. Gilbert looked up and down the coast, in cities such as Los Angeles and Palo Alto. He contacted therapists, evidence that he was looking for a family in crisis or at least one that had the habit of analysis. He interviewed dozens of families, but felt in each case that some essential ingredient was missing.

Three months into his search, having read *The Underground Man* (1971), a novel by Ross Macdonald that "perfectly described" the kind of family he was looking for, Gilbert decided to call up its author.[26] He and Alan Raymond were both fans of Macdonald's fiction. Macdonald's detective works, set in a fictionalized version of Santa Barbara, typically center on troubled affluent families whose wealth cannot compensate for their moral shortcomings. One critic has defined Macdonald's primary interest as "the family and its failures."[27] The narrator of *The Underground Man,* detective Lew Archer, is a divorced middle-aged man. Reviewing the novel in the *Los Angeles Times,* Robert Kirsch wrote that Macdonald examined California as "a microcosm of America," a notion that similarly motivated Gilbert's documentary.[28]

With Macdonald's help, Gilbert concentrated his search on Santa Barbara. In Lester's view, the producer was attracted to the visible contradictions of the city: "The University of California at Santa Barbara was the first place in which a bank was blown up in the 1960s. At the same time, the California headquarters of the John Birch Society is in Santa Barbara, and yet, on the surface, it's the most placid and beautiful town." As it was for Macdonald and other "hard-boiled" writers, the surface/depth contrast was important for Gilbert; the appearance of normalcy would work in his favor. Although he maintained that he wanted to explore relations between men and women, Lester recalled that they were not thinking about divorce or homosexuality as possible topics so much as the generation gap, the Vietnam War, and drug use.

Eventually, Santa Barbara started to look like the ideal location. Like Macdonald, Gilbert was keenly aware that the film and television industries, manufacturers of the programs that he felt embodied a misleading American dream, were also in Southern California. At the same time, there were other advantages to shooting the documentary there, advantages that motivated the film industry's move westward in the first decades of the century. The climate is generally mild and sunny, permitting location filming without the inconvenience of snow or rain. (Alan Raymond recalled that it rained just once during the seven months of location shooting.) People live outdoors as much as indoors, making it possible to shoot with available light under many circumstances. In addition, Santa Barbara had the advantage of being close to the largest film production center in the world, allowing for quick processing of the footage and easy repair of equipment.

An editor for the *Santa Barbara News-Press,* an acquaintance of Ross Macdonald, introduced Gilbert to the Louds. Bill and Pat were an attractive, outgoing, affluent couple with five children of various ages, the perfect family, from Gilbert's point of view. Bill owned his own company, and Pat raised the children in their spacious ranch-style home at 35 Wooddale Lane. It was crucial to the producer that Pat be a housewife. According to Reich's critique of American culture: "Wives of middle-class professional men occupy a particularly questionable position: well educated and highly intelligent, they are forced into a position in which they cannot do any real work or assume any real independence. When their children grow up, they are left with empty lives, and often there are divorces."[29] Gilbert had found his American family.

From James Day's perspective as president of NET, the family was not ideal because "it had more children than we counted on. It meant there would be more expense in covering the family. So, the budget went up the minute he found the Louds." Pat described Craig's first visit to her home in her autobiography *Pat Loud: A Woman's Story*:

> He sat down and explained about the series he had in mind, which was like one the BBC had made and another that had been done in Canada, and it would be a five-hour series showing five families across the country from California to New York. He called California the Last Frontier and said it was the setting most appropriate to "that most pervasive of fantasies, the American Dream." That was how he talked. He's full of this Eastern *angst*, and to Craig everything is pretty sad and terribly important and significant and has a lot to do with soul. He said he thought family life in the United States was embattled—disappearing, as a matter of fact—and he wanted to document it before it became completely obsolete."[30]

The producer talked much, but said little, of his intentions. Although she had misgivings, especially about her relationship with her husband, Mrs. Loud was proud of her family and thought the portrait would be flattering.

Pat and Bill Loud beside their pool in *An American Family*.

Shortly after their first encounter with Gilbert in May 1971, Pat and Bill Loud and the four of their children then living at home in Santa Barbara agreed to take part in the television program. The oldest Loud son, Lance, living in Manhattan at the time, also agreed. The shooting would begin in a matter of weeks.

▶

A Proposal for a Real-Life Soap Opera

A twenty-one-page proposal written by Craig Gilbert and Susan Lester shortly after filming started on *An American Family* offers the most concise record of the producer's intentions at the time. The fact that it was put together after Gilbert found the Louds demonstrates the importance he attached to choosing the right family. Lester joined the production team at this stage. Having just graduated from Douglas College at Rutgers University, she was working as a production secretary at NET when she met Gilbert. On the series, she earned $300 a week and received an associate producer's credit. Throughout his work on the program, Gilbert received the wage of a staff producer at NET, $750 a week plus benefits.[31]

Observational cinema does not lend itself to precise scripting or treatments, a fact that makes the style unpopular with funders. Before shooting, it was hard to define precisely what would be the substance of *An American Family*. Apart from the personalities of the family members, no one could predict what specific events would take place. Nevertheless, the proposal, like a script or novel from which a film is made, gives some indications of the producer's plans. Gilbert covered his bases in the proposal by mentioning numerous stylistic options and by exaggerating the historical scope of the series.

The ways in which the proposal differs from the actual documentary are as enlightening as the similarities between Gilbert's ideas and the finished product. The first sentence proposes "that National Educational Television produce a series of eight one-hour films covering the past and present lives of the William C. Loud family of Santa Barbara, California."[32] From the success of such TV series as *Victory at Sea* and *The Forsyte Saga* (1969–70), Gilbert knew that a weekly show had the potential to draw more viewers than a single program. The number of episodes was not clearly fixed, a fact that had serious consequences for the ultimate form of *An American Family*. The novelty of the idea made it difficult, if not impossible, for the producer to estimate the amount of footage to be shot, the months of location filming required, and the number of hours necessary to tell the story of the family. At every stage of production, Gilbert had to negotiate and justify expenses.[33] The lack of a predetermined length led to conflicts between Gilbert and the Louds as well as between Gilbert and the administration at WNET.

Gilbert and Lester's proposal promises to set the life of this real family "in a historical context which would also tell the story of the social and cultural changes that have taken place in the United States during the past fifty years."[34] This historical context is completely missing from the finished shows. Only episode four, in which Pat travels to visit her mother in Eugene, Oregon, and they reminisce about her childhood, focuses to any extent on the past. The other shows concentrate exclusively on the lives of the family members in the summer and fall of 1971. (One of the unfinished, and never shown, episodes featured Bill recounting his experiences in the navy during World War II.) There are no substantive references to the war in Vietnam, despite the fact that American Western Foundries, Mr. Loud's company, sold castings used by the U.S. military to pave roads there.[35] Certain trends, such as the baby boom and the suburbanization of American life, may be intuited from the program, but the so-called great events of contemporary history are all missing from *An American Family*. Even a soap opera such as *All My Children* (1970–present) dealt more directly with contemporary issues such as the Vietnam War.

The integration of these topics would have required a more conventional style than Gilbert used, perhaps including interviews with family members, expert voice-over narration, or even interviews with sociologists. With these issues in mind, Gilbert could have chosen a family with a son in Vietnam or a mother active in an antiwar organization. Gilbert's proposal to NET details a potpourri of contexts for understanding twentieth-century American life: the invention of radio; the stock market crash and the Great Depression; World War II; the arrival of television; the civil rights movement; the birth control pill and the polio vaccine; the assassinations of John Kennedy, Robert Kennedy, and Martin Luther King; the hippies; and the moon walk.

The proposal goes into detail about how the producers intended to achieve their goal of putting the family in this sociohistorical context. In addition to observational footage of the Louds, it mentions home movies and family photographs; "newsreel footage of events in which a member (or members) of the family participated"; news footage of events that affected the family; radio broadcasts the Louds recall hearing; radio broadcasts of events that touched the family; excerpts from fiction films and television programs of "special significance" for the Louds; popular songs, novels, plays, and articles familiar to the family; and, finally, "extended film interviews with every member of the immediate Loud family and with as many of its antecedents as are alive."[36] At least for the purposes of the treatment, Gilbert and Lester outline many stylistic options.

The proposal includes biographies of the Louds that extend beyond their nuclear family. The description of Pat contains more information about her deceased father—who fought in the Spanish-American War and worked as an engineer on the Panama Canal—than it does about her. Pat's brother Tom only appears in episode eight of *An American Family,* when Pat describes her reasons to divorce Bill, but the proposal points out that "Tom was sent with the 69th Division to Europe where he took part in the Battle of the Bulge and embraced the Russian Allies at the Elbe River." Like documentary theorist John Grierson before him, Gilbert believed that modern society was changing so rapidly that Americans were losing the ability to understand themselves. The proposal maintains that "in the past fifty years, both the content of change in this country and the media by which this change is transmitted have altered so greatly that the gap between parent and child seems to widen more profoundly each day."[37] Of course, grant proposals require something to justify their costs; it would be hard to imagine the producer arguing for a million-dollar program about the essentially static character of the American family.

Craig Gilbert did not make the series he described in his NET proposal. It is not clear at what stage his plan for setting the story of the family in a broader context was curbed, because the twelve-hour series offers less background than the twenty-one-page treatment. For the associate producer, writing the proposal amounted to developing the kernel of an original, intuitive idea—a dramatic nonfiction series about one family—and surrounding it with language that made the idea respectable to NET, CPB, and the Ford Foundation. Gilbert *was* genuinely interested in a historical perspective. In 1976, he circulated a proposal to the networks for a nonfiction program about one community over the century, "a series which, through the lives of eight or ten or twelve people living in a medium-sized midwestern city, would tell the story of what has happened to this country between the end of World War II and the present time."[38] But the drama of the Louds' separation, itself extremely topical, edged out other considerations, eliminating the producer's historical pretensions.

Having worked in the TV industry for his entire professional career, Gilbert was keenly aware of the role of serial drama in the history of both radio and television. He knew that viewers related documentaries not only to their own experiences but to other forms of broadcasting, fictional and nonfictional. The proposal deliberately brought together the conventions of daytime serials and those of social-issue documentary. With foresight, the producer recognized that for some audience members it would be of interest "simply as a real-life soap opera, the first of its kind in broadcasting history." He did not anticipate, however, that real-life soap opera would become the trademark term for *An American Family,* used by reviewers and viewers alike. For older viewers, Gilbert hoped the show would represent "an exercise in nostalgia—a trip backward in time to similar events in their own lives." He wanted the audience to see the program as "a series of mirrors in which young and old alike can begin to see themselves in relation to each other and to their society."[39]

The absence of a broader social context had serious implications for these goals. Had Gilbert incorporated more historical elements, the program would have been much less "like a soap opera." But in the editing room, the melodramatic focus of the footage won out over the comparative perspective of the proposal. Even television serials like *The Forsyte Saga* and, later, *Roots: The Triumph of an American Family* (1977) had stronger historical components than *An American Family.* Communication scholars Tamar Liebes and Elihu Katz note that the characters in *Dallas* (1978–91) appeared "afloat in space and time," and the same could be said—and was written at the time—of the Louds.[40] Many reviewers blamed the family, not the producer, for the lack of historical consciousness and connections to wider society in the program, as in Anne Roiphe's comment that fifteen-year-old Delilah Loud "never grieved for the migrant workers, the lettuce pickers, the war dead."[41] In the end, Gilbert was satisfied to portray a family *not* directly connected to the issues of the day in order to claim that Americans were alienated from politics and active citizenship. In his words, the Louds "don't communicate about the bad stuff. That's the way we are as a country, and that's what the series is about. We can't ever admit that we have made a mistake."[42]

[2] Filming the Louds, Editing the Footage

We felt relaxed around them, so it wasn't like letting a camera-person and soundperson in to film us, it's just that Susan and Alan were in the room.
:: Lance Loud

Once NET committed to produce *An American Family*, Gilbert did not have to worry constantly about fund-raising, an enviable position for a documentary producer in the United States, even though negotiations for the budget preoccupied him throughout production. On the basis of their work on *The Triumph of Christy Brown*, Gilbert hired Alan and Susan Raymond to shoot the series: "It's better to work with someone you know, but don't especially like, than to work with an unknown. At least I knew what I didn't like about the Raymonds. I also knew that by and large they would get it done if I could avoid killing them." For their skills, the Raymonds were well paid. According to the coordinating producer, Alan received $1,000 a week as cinematographer, and Susan was paid $900 a week for recording sound.[1] Alan maintains that he and Susan were the only people involved with *An American Family* who had any background in the observational style, having worked with Drew Associates and the Maysleses. In the spring of 1971, there were probably fewer than two dozen American filmmakers with substantial experience in this highly specialized form of documentary production.

Because filmmaking is a complex enterprise, it typically requires a division of labor and extensive collaboration. As producer, Craig Gilbert was responsible for conception, budgeting, finding the family, and, later, supervising the editing. Susan and Alan Raymond, for their part, contributed little to the editing stage. However, the Raymonds' role was central during the filming, whereas Gilbert's was, comparatively, peripheral. The film-

Alan and Susan Raymond filming at Santa Barbara High School.

makers' assertiveness and the producer's marginal role during the shooting led to tensions between them; their disagreements over authorship remain to this day unresolved.[2]

In her autobiography, Pat Loud recalled that they "fussed and stormed over their credits, and how they'd be billed, and if anybody was going to steal their thunder. Alan wanted to be credited as 'Director,' because it was he who chose what and when to film. Craig stubbornly refused because he said it would appear that we were being told what to do, and they finally arrived at the title of Filmmakers."[3] At one point, Susan and Alan declined to speak to Craig for several weeks. In Alan's view, "Interactions with Gilbert ranged from fistfights to not talking to one another for weeks on end. They were pretty hostile." Ironically, relations between Gilbert and the Raymonds were worse than those between the Louds; Pat and Bill never stopped speaking to one another during the shooting.

None of the disputes among crew members appears in the finished series, although Gilbert could have included them. In 1974, Michael Rubbo, a documentary filmmaker at the National Film Board of Canada, set out to film an interview with Fidel Castro in Cuba. *Waiting for Fidel* depicts how this plan disintegrates into a series of clashes among the Canadian producer of the film—a wealthy conservative businessman—the director Rubbo, and the socialist former premier of Newfoundland who accompanied them. Ensconced in a hotel in Havana, with the prospect of Castro's participation dwindling, the producer accuses Rubbo of waste and nonprofessionalism;

the making of the film becomes one of the subjects of the documentary. Gilbert, however, held to his "commitment to make *An American Family,* as far as possible, a series of films about the Louds and not about how the Louds interrelated with a film crew from NET."[4]

In the weeks before the shooting started, ground rules were established for the filming, as Gilbert recounted in a 1982 article titled "Reflections on *An American Family.*" Although the producer was unwilling to give the family editorial control over the finished series, he did agree that due to the delicate nature of the subject matter, "before any of the episodes were 'locked up,' the family or any member of the family would be allowed to see it and raise objections, which, I promised, would be listened to seriously and discussed fully, and changes would be made if they were warranted."[5] In practice, however, this agreement simply quelled the Louds' fears rather than giving them any specific input into the final form. Knowing that documentary filmmaking involves more than capturing "life as it is," Gilbert wanted to retain editorial control.

Few nonfiction filmmakers show their films to their subjects before they are finished, if at all. Frederick Wiseman, America's most prolific nonfiction producer, insists on his right to make films about other people's lives, repeatedly stating that he would never allow anyone else to have editorial

The NET production staff of *An American Family:* Jacqueline Donnet (coordinating producer), Alice Carey (production secretary), and Susan Lester (associate producer). Used by permission of *Studies in Visual Communication.*

control.[6] Alan Raymond shares this view, which he reiterated at a 1988 Museum of Broadcasting symposium devoted to *An American Family:* "I don't think that it's fair to say that subjects of a documentary have a right to see a film before it is finished. Most documentarians don't seek the opinions of their subjects." In the 1970s, allowing subjects to have any input was a relatively unorthodox practice. Recently, independent documentarists have increasingly experimented with more collaborative arrangements.[7]

The Louds signed releases to take part in a nonfiction series for public television. The ground rules included the agreement that "if the family or any member of the family wanted to be alone, all they had to do was go into a room and close the door." Under normal circumstances, filming was to take place between 8:00 A.M. and 10:00 P.M. Gilbert counseled the Louds: "They were to live their lives as if there were no camera present. They were to do nothing differently than they would ordinarily. This would be hard at first but would, I promised, become increasingly easier. We would never ask them to do anything just for the camera. In other words, we would never stage anything and we would never ask them to do or say something over again if we happened to miss it."[8] The Raymonds were not supposed to intrude on the lives of their subjects, to ask questions, conduct interviews, or otherwise direct events during the filming; they were to be as flies on the wall. By and large, the crew and the family stuck to this bargain for the long 216 days of shooting. By common agreement, the Louds received no payment for appearing in *An American Family.*

The observational style that Gilbert proposed marked a significant departure from standard television conventions, shooting practices that are still in force today. In *The Photographs of Chachaji: The Making of a Documentary Film,* essayist Ved Mehta describes the production of a WGBH-TV program. Most of the scenes in *Chachaji: My Poor Relation* (William Cran, 1980) were staged for the sake of being filmed and would not have taken place otherwise. Subjects were given explicit instructions by the director when to start and stop actions, activities that normally occurred in the morning were filmed in the early evening, sound effects were created on location by the director, actions were interrupted to allow for changes of camera angle, location settings were rearranged, and relatives of the protagonist were impersonated by others for the sake of convenience.[9]

TV scholar Roger Silverstone's *Framing Science: The Making of a BBC Documentary* corroborates Mehta's description of traditional nonfiction shooting practices. The subjects of *A New Green Revolution?* (Martin Freeth, 1984) were cued to begin certain activities when the crew was ready, interviewees were coached to respond in full sentences and to repeat their answers, subjects were asked to change their clothing, settings were rearranged, actions were repeated, and sound effects were created in the dubbing studio. The interview passages used in the final film were, according to Silverstone, "as unlike everyday conversation as any kind of talk can possibly be."[10] As in the case of *Chachaji: My Poor Relation*, extensive and authoritative voice-over commentary tied together the various threads of the program.

An American Family required not only the cooperation of the Louds, but extensive collaboration among crew members. The logistics of shooting an observational documentary of such a scale were daunting. Jacqueline Donnet, an old friend of Gilbert, coordinated the work of the location managers who supervised the shooting. She worked as the production stage manager for John Houseman while he was artistic director of the Professional Theatre Group at UCLA before embarking on her career in public television. As coordinating producer, Donnet received $450 a week. She joined the production team after the Louds agreed to take part in the series. "My main function as the coordinating producer was basically to keep track of the money, the 16mm film, and Lance," she recalled. Because Lance Loud was living in New York City, where the production office was located, Donnet spoke to him regularly. "He was very nice about it. He used to call me every morning and I'd say, 'Lance, what are you doing today?' He'd say, 'Oh, I don't know.' And then half an hour later he'd call to say he was going to the Metropolitan Museum of Art!" In practice, this meant that if Pat Loud went on a trip, as seen in episode four, someone had to purchase plane tickets, reserve hotel rooms for the crew, and secure permission in advance to shoot on location wherever they were going.

As the footage came in from the West Coast, Donnet arranged to have the film and magnetic sound track synchronized, more than 730 reels of 16mm. She created a library for this material in addition to the home movies, photographs, and memorabilia that the Louds lent to NET. The staff sorted and cataloged boxes of family mementos: bills, receipts, birthday cards, report cards, and notes. Gilbert hoped to use this material to fill in the history of the family. The library also included some fifty reels, thirty-three hours, of Super-8mm footage of Lance in New York City and Europe, shot by a separate crew. At NET, Donnet had the help of Alice Carey, the production secretary, who had worked extensively in underground theater, and became, in her words, "the liaison between the straight population of Channel 13—anybody who was terrified of the word *homosexual*—and Lance." Born in Manhattan and educated in English literature at New York University, Carey claimed she was "overqualified to work on *An American Family*" but "needed the money." Carey knew drag queen Jackie Curtis as well as the other cast members of *Vain Vic-*

tory, the transvestite performers whom Lance takes his mother to see in episode two.[11] Carey did extensive archival research for the project and received $250 a week.

The shooting of *An American Family* began when Pat Loud arrived in New York City in late May 1971 to visit Lance at the Chelsea Hotel. Gilbert and the Raymonds knew the milieu of the Chelsea better than Pat did.[12] During this visit, the producer discovered that Lance was gay, "a ready-made point of tension," in Gilbert's words.[13] The Raymonds started filming Mrs. Loud at the hotel before they had even been introduced. Pat's self-consciousness did not let up for weeks and probably contributed to her reserved character in the series. She held back her emotions in reaction to the camera, "that eye of half-truth. It scared me at first. I didn't know what to do with it."[14] However difficult it was for the Louds to learn to live with a camera crew, it was stranger for the Raymonds. As Susan noted: "We were living their lives completely. I can't stress that enough. We couldn't even plan when we wanted to eat. Imagine what it's like to live according to someone else's schedule for eight months! When we finished, we felt a little like soldiers returning to civilian life. We almost had to learn how to plan our own lives all over again."[15]

Documentary shooting involves balancing technical considerations with the need to interact with others. Observational filmmakers do not only observe. Off-camera, they speak to their subjects, get to know them, share stories, and find points in common. As the months went by, the Raymonds practically became members of the family. Mrs. Loud even offered the young couple a room to stay in. As she put it, "We really liked and cared about each other."[16] Alan took credit for facilitating this rapport: "Going into a family's household to film is very difficult psychologically. Whatever was Craig's ultimate contribution to the series, he did not get the family to be relaxed in front of the camera; that was our contribution." Craig Gilbert and Pat Loud, too, became good friends.[17] "Craig was always an ultra-angst-ridden, guilty, white, liberal guy, a nice guy," according to Lance. "He represented this sensitive intellectual whom my mom felt that she needed at that point." Everyone involved agreed that the Raymonds would never have been able to shoot candid material of the Louds if the production team had not developed close personal friendships with the family members. The size of the crew facilitated this process; on most occasions, Susan and Alan were the only crew members present during the filming.

"That was the real secret behind *An American Family*," Lance later asserted:

The reason it was made, the reason they got the shots, the reason we opened up to them, was because a very strong bond was formed between the family and Alan, Susan, and [assistant cameraman] Tom Goodwin. We opened up to them because they really became extremely close with us. The big question we are always asked is, "How could you let the cameras into your life?" Well, it really wasn't the case of letting the cameras into our lives. It meant adjusting our family to include these three or four extra people who were young, very simpatico, very cool, and hip. And very nice at the same time, having qualities of being both very intelligent, and informed about the world, yet being very homey. We felt relaxed around them, so it wasn't like letting a cameraperson and soundperson in to film us, it's just that Susan and Alan were in the room.

Nevertheless, the filmmakers' outsider status guaranteed that the footage would be more than just home movies; they were simultaneously involved and detached.

Like Mr. and Mrs. Loud, the Raymonds were married; they could understand the rewards and difficulties of marriage. In age, however, they were closer to the children. In 1971, Alan was twenty-six years old and Susan was twenty-four; Lance, the eldest of the Loud children, was twenty. Furthermore, Alan could identify with the boys and their concerns, and Susan could relate comfortably to the girls' experiences. During the seven-month shoot, the filmmakers learned the nuances of the family's interactions. There were limits, however, to relations between crew and family members. Pat became friends with Susan Lester, confiding in her about her relationship with Bill. In July, Alan complained that this friendship interfered with the filming and requested that Gilbert remove the associate producer. Craig later recalled that Lester "agreed that, very likely, her long conversations with Pat had made it difficult for Alan Raymond to do his job. She added that if there had to be a choice . . . between maintaining a friendship and the integrity of the film, she would opt for the friendship every time."[18] The producer, for his part, believed the crew should stay out of the affairs of the Louds, at least during the shooting. To minimize her effect on the family, he sent Lester back to Manhattan to research the historical context for the series. "We still harbored the idea that we might put some other kinds of footage around them," she remembered. "I got very much enmeshed with the family archive."

During this period, the Louds were also observing the Raymonds. Lance noted a pattern to the crew's interaction: "Susan usually worked as the goodwill ambassador. She's the person who talked to the people, warmed them up, got them kind of relaxed, and was very friendly, while Alan was brooding behind the camera. Then, later on, he got to be friendly, too." Balancing the demands of technology and sociability was not a simple task; the use of the sophisticated camera and sound equipment had to become second nature. The Raymonds' performance demanded considerably more than that of the Louds.

The filmmakers had to maintain a difficult dual consciousness, being both involved (interacting and caring) and removed (observing and recording). Although technological breakthroughs set the stage for synchronous sound shooting, observational cinema stands for a mode of production and a style invented by people, not by equipment. New gear made it possible, and the subjectivity and skill of the filmmakers made it meaningful. It is difficult to appreciate fully the heavy technological mediation involved in such work. Good verité footage represents the fragile end product of a series of complex technical maneuvers. A description of the circumstances and practical choices for the style of *An American Family* highlights the Raymonds' talent.

▶

Choreography of Camera and Sound

Observational cinema would not have been possible without a series of technical innovations that took place in the late 1950s. Stefan Kudelski's Nagra tape recorder appeared in 1959 and, together with lightweight noiseless 16mm cameras, paved the way for portable synchronous shooting. Crystal-governed motors, first employed by Drew Associates, kept the cameras and tape recorders running at an extremely consistent speed for synchronization. Faster lenses, and more light-sensitive film stocks, allowed cinematographers to shoot with available light, and the development of the zoom lens let them change the frame without moving. Ultra-directional portable microphones offered recordists greater opportunity to isolate sounds in a given scene. Through the efforts of documentary filmmakers in the United States, France, and Canada, by the middle 1960s the filming apparatus could for the first time be subordinated to events occurring in front of it.

Susan and Alan Raymond were able to move independent of one another and still obtain perfect synchronization of image and sound. Each was free to approach a scene separately, although in practice they moved in unison, anticipating each other's movements as well as those of the family members. Alan used an Eclair NPR 16mm camera with a 12/120mm Angenieux zoom lens; the zoom gave Raymond the flexibility to employ the full panoply of image size from close-up to long shot. Susan used primarily Sennheiser 805 shotgun and 404 omnidirectional microphones, together with Sony ECM-16 mikes, Vega wireless lavalieres, and telephone taps. The ECM-16s were installed around the house, with cables, in inaccessible areas: "The most successful planted mike was in the chandelier over the dining room table where as many as six people were recorded while eating, using only the small Sony ECM-16." The sound was recorded on one-quarter-inch magnetic tape with a Nagra IV. Using a special BS-II preamp, Susan was able to operate, and mix, three microphones simultaneously while in the home.[19] Her virtuoso performance was worthy of Robert Altman's multitrack sound innovations of the same period. Despite all these complex technological maneuvers, during the filming, the Raymonds came across to the Louds as human beings, not as machines for image and sound reproduction.

Susan Raymond used a shotgun microphone because it allowed for selective recording of the environment, enabling her to foreground certain sounds while relegating others to the background. Instructions for location recordists include standing as close as possible to the subject without appearing in the frame. Observational cinematographers prefer viewfinders, such as that on Raymond's Eclair, which allow them to see beyond the frame of the image, the perfect space for the roving mike. In this way, the cinematographer has a constant view of the microphone and the location of the soundperson, while the viewer never sees either. In Alan's opinion, "The camera/sound team must develop a kind of choreography where both parties are aware of each other all the time. The cameraman must listen to the dialogue and the sound recordist must watch what the cameraman is shooting."[20] Or, as Susan has described their technique, "It's like Fred and Ginger dancing, we each can anticipate the next move."[21] The wireless microphones that she used allowed for even greater flexibility than the shotgun mikes. Extremely small and unobtrusive, designed to be worn on the chests of individual speakers, these microphones reproduce the human voice with great fidelity at the expense of the ambient sound. The Raymonds believe that technically difficult, and ethically sensitive, scenes, such as arguments Bill and Pat had in restaurants, would have been impossible to film without the wireless lavalieres.[22]

Although it would have been feasible to shoot almost exclusively with available light using black-and-white film, the decision to use color obliged the Raymonds to add artificial illumination. (*An American Family* was one of the first observational films shot in color; Wiseman did not use color stock until 1982.) Five-hundred-watt quartz bulbs replaced the regular lights in the Loud's twelve-room home. On sunny days in Santa Barbara, Alan could film indoors without any artificial illumination. Raymond used a Minolta Autospot light meter to measure light levels from a distance without disturbing the subjects. "Nothing, I might add, unnerves someone more than to stick a Spectra meter in his face. Actors are used to it, real people are not."[23] Although Alan had to remember at all times what filter he had on the camera, he still managed to make the Louds feel comfortable, just as they made him feel welcome in their home.

Although the zoom lens gives a greater range of options than a fixed-focal-length lens, some cinematographers, such as Raymond, do not like zooming in the middle of a shot.

> I usually worked fairly far back from my subjects and tried not to do too much zooming if I reframed or panned from one person to another. Instead of changing the focal length of the zoom, I would follow focus, trying to minimize the psychological effect of emphasis which the zoom shot always gives. I also avoided the extreme close-up which I feel creates false tension and is overused in this kind of filmmaking. I like to include backgrounds and favor the medium shot. In this way, I let the audience make the choice between watching a person's facial expression or his "body language," which often reveals more of what people are unconsciously doing or feeling.[24]

Like many documentary cinematographers, Raymond preferred to rely on wide shots, composition in depth, and relatively long takes. At the same time, however, he made sure to obtain coverage of each scene for maximum flexibility during editing. If the Louds looked intently at something in the scene, Alan remembered to get a shot from their angle of view. In the middle of most events, he changed his position to obtain reverse angle shots. In addition, the cinematographer followed cues the Louds provided in their conversations, so that he could supply visual matches, especially in the use of detail shots. Because Susan kept the recorder running while Alan reframed, continuous sound facilitated the maintenance of spatial and temporal relations in the cutting stage.

It is much more difficult to shoot observational scenes than fictional ones. The documentary cameraperson must perform the work of several individuals by taking light meter readings, framing, following focus, panning, and tracking unpredictable actions. On a Hollywood set, these jobs are performed separately by different members of the crew, including the director of photography, the focus puller, and the camera operator, all of whom usually have precise information about the predetermined movements of the actors. Observational cinematographers enjoy special pleasure and anxiety in recording events that occur spontaneously. Independent documentarist Ross McElwee described the anguish involved in filming his autobiographical documentary *Sherman's March* (1986): "Every night you go home and pull out your hair and say, 'I missed it. God, I didn't get it.'"[25]

Michel Negroponte, cinematographer and director of the independent documentaries *Silver Valley* (1983) and *Jupiter's Wife* (1995) has stated:

"If you think something interesting is about to happen, start filming. If it doesn't happen, stop. You can make that decision after thirty seconds, but if it's working, keep shooting." With the generous NET budget, the Raymonds were not obliged to stop filming if nothing was happening, "We tended to shoot complete 400' [eleven-minute] rolls rather than short bursts. People reveal themselves within the long run of the magazine rather than in short fragmented shots."[26] Observational shooting requires a kind of sixth sense, shared between the cinematographer and the sound recordist, about the significance of events on location. Alan and Susan's expertise became automatic, allowing them to shoot with the same facility as a writer taking notes with pen and paper. As Gilbert predicted, the Louds gradually became comfortable with the presence of the Raymonds; this was the rationale for the unusually long shooting schedule. According to Pat, Bill "adored being filmed—he basked in it. He was the only one who ever *asked* to be filmed."[27] Mr. Loud stated on *The Dick Cavett Show* that he considered the presence of the crew akin to having "a maid in the house," an unintended compliment to the "fly on the wall" approach.

The Raymonds eventually learned that if they missed certain scenes, they might nevertheless have a second chance, because the length of the shoot virtually guaranteed that comparable situations would arise again. The emphasis of the observational style on singular events was mitigated by the repetitiveness of everyday life. Bill Loud singled out this dimension of the documentary in an article for the *Chicago Tribune*. "When viewing the many segments of film before they were cut into a series," he recalled, "one of my deepest impressions was of the repetitious, seven-day week, 24-hour day we all live."[28] The seven-month shoot meant that the crew could potentially record several hundred breakfast scenes. The coordinating producer recalled, "Alan Raymond finally decided that it really didn't make very much difference if he ran out of film during an argument, for example, because, in all likelihood, a week later that same underlying problem would resurface." Nonfiction producers rarely have the luxuries of time and money to allow for such thorough recording. A TV crew may spend half an hour interviewing someone for the evening news, and another team might spend half a day filming an interview for a feature documentary. The Raymonds, on the other hand, shot three hundred hours of footage, an average of an hour and a half each day for seven months. This schedule gave the Raymonds time to get to know each family member's traits and habits. Particularly interested in capturing insights into character, which he and Susan discussed at length when they were not on location, Alan asserted, "What's really important is how people relate to one another. That's what good dramatic films are about, that's what all good fiction is about."[29]

As the shooting progressed, the Louds sensed that their lives were being acted out upon a stage greater than their living room. When her relationship with Bill disintegrated, Pat took solace from "living a story that had to be told, and the story was building to a climax. It was just as Craig had said: The truths that were lurking under the surface were now ready to explode into view."[30] The main crises in their lives were also moments when the bond between crew and family was strained. Pat refused to be filmed when she informed her children of her decision to file for a divorce. Additionally, she did not want her encounter with her brother and sister-in-law in early September to be recorded:

> *I* thought I made it perfectly clear that I *didn't* want the scene with Tom and Yvonne filmed, because the next day I was going to tell Bill and I knew that that night I was really going to let my hair down. I kind of put it in the same category as talking to the kids, essentially too private for the series. Embattled Pat, the ailing wife, was about to make a stand, at last. But what do you know, there in Tom's living room were Craig and Charlotte Zwerin and Alan Raymond and Tommy Goodwin, looking sheepish, setting up lights and getting the camera ready. I was stunned, and Craig and I tore off to the bedroom where we had an emotion-charged exchange and I said I hadn't agreed to let him film it and he said I *had*.[31]

Pat acquiesced, and the conversation was filmed. Obviously a pivotal scene, it takes up almost thirty minutes of episode eight.

Whereas certain actions occurred with monotonous regularity, others happened just once. So the Raymonds had to be prepared to film at all times. The night of September 3, when Pat asked Bill to move out of the house, was the "most dramatic action we filmed," Alan maintained.

> The whole family was shattered. I'm going in and out the door with Bill, and Pat's in the back room crying, and the kids are wandering around the house in a state of shock. I'm faced with a tremendous responsibility and the knowledge that this is a one-time-only event. I have the responsibility not only to physically record it, by which I mean get an exposure and get some sound, but also to get a sense of the drama, the human drama that's unfolding. In documentary filmmaking, that's probably the equivalent of landing the space shuttle.

The Louds were responsible for living their lives; the Raymonds were responsible for recording them. "By this time," Pat remembered, "almost a million dollars had been poured into filming the Louds. I felt an obligation to live up to our part of the bargain, which was, of course, to try to be as honest and candid as we normally would be had the cameras *not* been there."[32] Once the filming was set in motion, the family never seriously considered dropping out of the project. The involvement and detachment of the filmmakers appears clearly in the honesty of Alan's

Pat Loud in her bedroom in episode nine of *An American Family.*

recollection; the Louds' family crisis represents a high point in Raymond's professional career.

The Louds' decision to separate caused logistical problems for Gilbert because he felt he needed two crews to cover the separate activities of Bill and the rest of the family. He hired cinematographer Joan Churchill and sound recordist Peter Pilafian to film Bill after he moved to the Lemon Tree Motel in Santa Barbara. Churchill and Pilafian each received $1,000 a week.[33] With another team filming Lance in New York City and Europe, this meant that three separate crews were, for part of the production, shooting concurrently. In addition, the crew provided Kevin Loud with a Super-8mm camera for his trip to Southeast Asia. Gilbert initially hoped to include this amateur footage in the documentary, but none was used. Hiring a second California crew led to bitter fights between the producer and the Raymonds, who believed they could adequately cover the entire family after the separation. These additional expenses also had to be justified to a skeptical WNET administration.

The crew traveling in Europe with Lance Loud during his summer vacation used experimental Super-8mm equipment, a Nizo S56 camera and Sony TC 124 tape recorder, modified for synchronous sound by Albert Mecklinberg, one of the designers working with Richard Leacock at the Massachusetts Institute of Technology.[34] Terry eventually shot forty thousand feet of Super-8mm film, approximately thirty-three hours. Some of this footage was blown up to 16mm to be edited into *An American Family.*

Lance and John Terry became friends. As the cinematographer remarked, "It's really hard to film someone you don't like. I don't have much interest in doing it." Lance recalled the shoot in Europe: "I was bottoming out at poverty level. As filmmakers, they had money. They were filming me being poor and they really couldn't tread upon the naturalism of the scene by giving me money. But they took us to dinner from time to time." Terry and Mecklinberg each received $1,000 a week for filming Lance in New York City, Copenhagen, and Paris.

The size of the production made for a broad division of labor, with several crews, location managers, and numerous production assistants. During the shooting, Gilbert, Lester, Goodwin, and the location managers stayed at the Miramar Beach Hotel in Santa Barbara. (The Raymonds lived separately from the rest of the NET production staff, renting a house from the actor John Ireland, just ten minutes by car from the Louds' home. They declined Pat's offer to take a room in her house, preferring to retain some independence from the family.) Pat remembered watching the rushes at the seaside hotel: "They had rooms on the beach and also a bungalow that served as a production room. There each day's shooting was screened as soon as it was returned from processing in Los Angeles. We went there several times to see certain footage we were particularly interested in, and sometimes we were specifically invited."[35] Having already experienced the actions seen in the rushes, the Louds quickly tired of viewing the raw footage.

The shooting of *An American Family* brought together a group of New York City media professionals and an upper-middle-class family from Southern California. Postproduction, however, was entirely in the hands of the WNET crew. The Louds went from being real people to being images on celluloid, figures to be watched, transcribed, occasionally discarded, and eventually edited into twelve episodes of a nonfiction television series. Although the family knew the producer, the cinematographers, and the sound recordists firsthand, the editors were strangers.

▶
_____

Editing: Less Is More

> *The problem with public television is that there are no commercials.*
> :: Jacqueline Donnet, coordinating producer

Documentary filmmakers often have difficulty knowing when to stop shooting. Many are simply forced to quit when they run out of funds or time. Such choices are part of the work of mediation, of transforming actuality into representation. Craig Gilbert decided, arbitrarily, to cease filming the Louds on the last day of 1971. "Even if Pat Loud's mother died on January 2, we would not be there to film," Donnet noted. Pat recalled their departure: "On December 31, 1971, seven months after it started, the series was suddenly over, and they all packed up their cameras, their lights, their sound equipment, their problems, concerns, and what had been, for me, their magic, and they left."[36] Gilbert checked out of the Miramar Beach Hotel and returned to Manhattan to work on the editing. The Raymonds took an extended vacation in Hawaii to recuperate from the shooting. "After the experience of *An American Family*," Susan stated, "we vowed we'd never work for anyone else again, that we would do it ourselves. Be our own producers and live or die on whatever the work turned out to be."

The Louds went back to their daily activities, as yet relatively unchanged by the experience of being filmed for seven months. The broadcast, not the shooting, radically transformed their private lives. If the footage had been destroyed at WNET in 1972, the American public would not have heard of the Louds. As it turned out, the airing of *An American Family* made them celebrities, and this changed their lives forever. Pat anticipated this and reflected on the coming broadcast: "In some way I would change. That's what the series had always been supposed to do for us."[37]

Initially, the producer hoped the editing might proceed in tandem with the shooting, keeping down the costs of production. Editing during production, a rapid connect-the-dots approach, usually occurs with storyboarded fiction films under tight deadlines. Given Gilbert's indecision about the final form of the program, it is surprising he considered it. While still searching for a family, Gilbert hired Charlotte Zwerin, a veteran New York editor of documentaries, to supervise the cutting.[38] Zwerin provided a hedge against Gilbert's insecurity about the series. In his opinion, Zwerin was "single-handedly responsible" for the success of *Gimme Shelter* (1970), the Maysleses' film about the Rolling Stones, for which she was credited as codirector. She questioned Gilbert's decision to hire Alan and Susan Raymond, imploring him to have the Maysles brothers shoot the film. The Raymonds were not fond of Zwerin. Once filming began, Gilbert decided to delay the editing until everything had been shot, processed, and viewed in its entirety. In September 1971, he suggested Zwerin return to New York City to talk to additional editors.

According to Gilbert, Zwerin made oral commitments to three editors without his knowledge. All three were women, editing being one of the few positions in the industry in which women had consistently found work. In addition to feeling his role undermined, the producer believed that *An American Family*, conceived as a series about the relations between

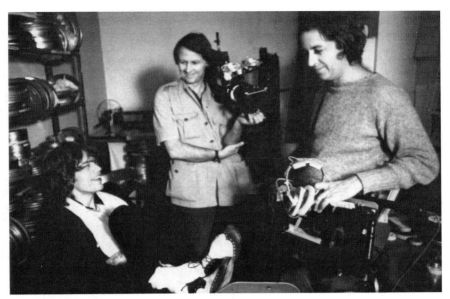

Publicity still of Mick Jagger and the Maysles brothers for *Gimme Shelter*.

men and women, should be edited by a team that included both. Tempers flared among Gilbert, Zwerin, and the WNET management. Gilbert flew east for a meeting and Zwerin quit when he refused to honor the commitments she had made.

Eleanor Hamerow, one of the three editors Zwerin had lined up, was eventually hired to work on the series, only to be fired by Gilbert after completing the first episode. "I don't think she'll agree to anything that I'm saying," coordinating producer Donnet recalled, "but the simple thing is that she hated the family." The producer felt that Hamerow was struggling to remake the series in the editing room. She cut the footage against the grain, fighting her feelings of dislike for the Louds, rather than following the lead of the material. According to Gilbert, Hamerow came from a school of filmmaking that believes meaning is created in the editing room, whereas the observational style, relying more on a long-take aesthetic, privileges shooting.[39] It remains unclear precisely how Hamerow influenced the show, but episode one is the most didactic, and least flattering, view of the family, especially from the point of view of editing. Ironically, given Gilbert's stated intentions, *An American Family* ended up being edited by a team of men: David Hanser, Pat Cook, and Ken Werner. Eleanor Hamerow received the editing credit for episode one.

The principal editor for the series was David Hanser. He and the others received $800 a week for their work, union wages in 1972. Hanser grew up and attended high school in Westchester County, New York. After having graduated from the Pratt Institute in Brooklyn, he entered the army and served in Korea after the armistice. Throughout the 1960s, Hanser free-lanced for the news departments of the three commercial networks, working on such series as *World War One* (1964–65) and *CBS Reports.* At WNDT and NET, he edited cultural documentaries about artists such as painter Andy Warhol. Having heard about *An American Family* in the halls of National Educational Television, he approached the producer in late 1971 to ask if he could work on it. Like Gilbert, Hanser was trained on a variety of mostly nonfiction TV shows.

The editing process took more than a year and involved a team of people working under the supervision of Gilbert and series editor Hanser. During February, March, and April 1972, Gilbert, Hanser, Hamerow, Lester, and Donnet watched all three hundred hours of 16mm film of the Loud family. They found themselves, six hours a day for three straight months, vicariously experiencing the lives of the Louds. Hours of break-fasts, lunches, and dinners swirled by on the screen. Donnet remembered that the team "used to run into those eating scenes just prior to our lunch break, so watching made us very hungry." During the viewing of the rushes, they took extensive notes; the transcripts were as thick as several New York City telephone books.

The level of identification of the editing team with the family was comparable to the dual consciousness of the Raymonds. The editors lived vicariously through characters in ways that audiences would later, too. "Slowly but surely," Gilbert recalled, "the lives of the people on the screen started becoming more real than our own; without even being aware of it we found ourselves using words and phrases common to the Louds and talking about family situations as if we had actually participated in them."[40] Bill Loud tended to refer to people by their last names, so the members of the WNET production team adopted this practice. Donnet, never having met the Louds in person, felt that the most disturbing sensation was "the fact that we had gotten to know these people very, very well. All of their stories, their foibles, their history."

Like viewers of Andy Warhol's films, the producers discovered that watching footage shot in real time was strangely unlike real life. For Alice Carey, "It was boring. It was boring. It was long! I've got to hand it to David Hanser, the editor, because they put the camera on the Louds for everything." The scale of the documentary was unprecedented. Hanser re-called that he "felt that the project was over after having finished screening the dailies." Gilbert deliberately hired editors who had no personal contact with the Louds. He wanted them to react to what was on the screen, not to their memories of the shoot or to their knowledge of the family. For the editors, the only reality was the 16mm footage. Hanser, Hamerow, Werner, and Cook became the first audience of *An American Family*.

For Gilbert, the role of the editors was to do justice to the footage on its own terms. Richard Leacock, a brilliant cinematographer who developed the observational shooting style, believes the opposite: that only someone present during the shooting can assure, through the editing, the authenticity of the events as they happened.[41] In this, Gilbert is a constructivist, whereas Leacock is an empiricist. Tom Haneke, editor of Barbara Kopple's *American Dream* (1990)—a documentary about labor strife at a Hormel meatpacking plant in Minnesota—echoes Gilbert's perspective: "I'm really the viewer surrogate the first time I see the film. Sometimes right after the crew comes back from location, we screen the dailies. I don't care how good you are, you can't completely eliminate the feelings you had when you were on location filming the event."[42] From the perspective of the editor, fiction or documentary, if it is not in the footage, it did not happen. Geof Bartz, editor of George Butler's *Pumping Iron* (1977)—a nonfiction study of professional bodybuilding featuring Arnold Schwarzenegger—has stated, "The editor is the surrogate audience, the person who doesn't have feelings about the characters based on whether or not they like the actors, whether they are nice people or not, but simply how they are in the film. You have to pretend that you are the audience."[43]

Hanser joined the project as the screening of the rushes was in progress.

Editors of *An American Family:* Ken Werner, Pat Cook, and David Hanser. Used by permission of *Studies in Visual Communication.*

Like the others, he was powerfully drawn into the lives of people he had never met. Lance was the only family member Hanser encountered in person during the editing stage; he was hired to help the assistant editors identify people in the footage. "I would see Lance for hours on the screen," Hanser recalled, "and then, during lunch, go upstairs and see him in person. Reality began to get blurred." Hanser took a keen interest in the material because he himself was getting divorced while working on the series. He shared some of Gilbert's pessimism about relations between men and women.

After viewing three months' worth of rushes, the production team discussed how the material might be edited into episodes. There were different opinions about how to organize the documentary. The team considered devoting an individual show to each member of the family. Ultimately, Gilbert chose a chronological format in which individual incidents would form the basis for sequences and shows. Only the first episode contradicted this format, showing the end first, as what Hanser called a "tease." Donnet acknowledged that the idea to begin with the last day of filming was "a major editorial decision." In this respect, as well as others, the first hour differs from the rest. It introduces the family members and contrasts their lives before and after the parents' separation.

The series could have been organized differently; no blueprint existed for editing three hundred hours of nonfiction footage into an indeterminate

Lance Loud in Central Park, New York City, in *An American Family*.

number of programs. Episodes based on individual family members would have radically altered both the structure (single protagonists rather than multiple-focus narrative) and the way the program was watched (audiences may not have remained loyal if the focus shifted from show to show). Furthermore, viewers might have adopted different positions vis-à-vis the Loud family if the program had not opened with the denouement. Bill and Pat's impending separation would not have hung over every minute of *An American Family* as it did.

Starting the series on New Year's Eve solved the producer's search for an opening scene. Gilbert had no "natural" opening like the end point provided by the celebration of the New Year; the flashback structure set up the last day of filming as the end and the beginning. Furthermore, one practical reason for calling attention to the end in the first show was that no one knew the total number of episodes. In a June 1972 memo to the WNET administration, Gilbert maintained that the structure and length could be established only in the editing room—wishful thinking for a television producer.[44] Whereas John Jay Iselin, the new station president, and Robert Kotlowitz, the new vice president of programming, were content to have eight episodes, Gilbert thought that he needed fifteen to do the story justice.[45] Twelve was a compromise, although the producer was given permission to look for outside funding for shows thirteen, fourteen, and fifteen.[46] Putting the outcome in the first hour guaranteed that the final part of the story got fully told, just in case Gilbert was not allowed to make all the episodes he wanted. Like a journalist who composes his story with the most important information in the first sentence, Gilbert opened the documentary with the last day of filming to highlight the breakup of the Louds.

The editors had to invent a structure for seven months in the life of a family. One of the most difficult decisions was when to end one show and begin another. Rough-cut sequences, individual scenes, moved from one episode to another. Hanser saw the cutting of observational footage not as a process of assembling, montage, or construction, but as a process of "stripping away." Like editors of fiction and documentary alike, he tried not to impose his own feelings about the family members on the material. Whether he felt that Bill was awful for cheating on Pat was, from his point of view, irrelevant; they were characters on celluloid. Hanser's collaboration with Gilbert went more smoothly than had that of the Raymonds; as he recalled, "Everybody was really trying to follow the lines that Craig had laid out." Gilbert and the editors worked to strike a balance between sequences that caught the flavor of everyday life and other more riveting material.

Overall, Hanser was pleased with the rushes. Although shot primarily with one camera, most events were covered fully, with reaction shots and cutaways that allowed for considerable flexibility in the editing. For example, if the Loud family spent an hour at breakfast one morning, the Raymonds might shoot three rolls of 16mm film. With these thirty-three minutes of footage, the editors had ample material to piece together a fluid sequence. In other cases, Hanser and company were excited to discover that separate crews had recorded both sides of several telephone conversations, allowing for crosscutting between family members. The film library created for the series by Donnet, Lester, and Carey greatly facilitated this process. "I must say that the organization for putting together the series was immaculate," Donnet remembered. "After all that footage came through, we didn't lose a frame, and that's unusual. One could go back very quickly and say, 'Remember that time that Grant stood on top of the car at the rally'—or whatever one wanted—and one could find it instantly. One could really almost read the camera reports."

Hanser's approach to cutting was guided by concerns for smooth continuity:

> When you edit something like that you have to look at it, listen to it, and try to pick out the things that are most revealing about the people and that further the story. If somebody says what they're going to do that night, that might be useful, depending on what else is there. So you try to make sure to include that in the editing, because you're trying to tell the story without any narration. You want to let the people provide their own information about the story.

Like Hollywood screenwriters, observational editors learn to provide expository information in the words of their characters. At the same time, the cutters kept an eye out for especially dramatic scenes. "Of course," Hanser added, "if there was something really funny or emotional that took place, an emotionally charged exchange between two people, you made sure that was part of the sequence."

Observational editing techniques follow continuity conventions—establishing shots, match on action cut-ins, eye-line matches, point-of-view shots, and the like—established in the film industry during the silent era. At that time, Hollywood companies developed elaborate means of maintaining continuity through supervision of scripts, props, lighting, performance, and shooting style, means typically unavailable to documentary filmmakers. Such continuity conventions make it difficult to edit together actuality material shot at different times. Continuity requires a consistency of space, time, action, and character that, in the case of *An American Family*, was best suited by the adoption of a sequential approach. "We had to tell it chronologically," Donnet noted, "because otherwise someone has long hair in one shot and short hair in the next." For these reasons, observational films often follow the order in which they were shot. Documentary editors do not necessarily believe that chronology best represents actual experience, but a particular system of narrative causality leads them to tell stories in the order in which they were recorded.

Although chronology remained the governing paradigm for the editing of *An American Family*, scene changes often involved shifts from one member of the family to another in a different place at a different time. "They were a good family," Donnet remarked, "because they moved around a lot. They didn't sit still too long." Seven different family members, and footage from as many as three different crews working simultaneously, allowed for a multiple-focus narrative structure that was not simply linear. "When the editors used to say, 'I've run out of something' or 'This is getting really boring and nobody is going to stay with this scene much longer,' then it was very convenient to have Lance running around New York," Donnet observed. "So we cut to Lance taking a bath or whatever he's doing and then we go back to the family. The problem with public television is there are no commercials. We had to link everything up and that was very difficult to do. On network television, the scene ends, the commercial comes on, and then you can start fresh somewhere else."

■————————————————————————————————

Reshooting

Although they were committed to an observational style, when necessary, the production team resorted to other methods. The performance of *Vain Victory* at La Mama Theater in episode two was not filmed on the evening that Lance and his mother attended. It was shot later, by another crew, after the show had moved to a different theater. In addition, the Raymonds filmed an on-camera introduction by Gilbert in Santa Barbara in 1972. The filmmakers also returned to the West Coast to shoot an exterior of the Loud's home. "We couldn't find a single shot of the house," Donnet recalled. "It didn't exist. They didn't hold them long enough. Editors always scream at the camerapeople about this kind of stuff." David Hanser came "down the street about three blocks away from where our offices were at 10 Columbus Circle because he felt so bad he couldn't say it on the phone. He walked over and he said, 'You won't believe this, but we don't have a shot of the house.' Of course Craig and I said, 'That's absurd. We've seen that house for days.' But there wasn't one that was held long enough to use."

Observational filmmakers do not, as a rule, use prerecorded or scored music or sound effects in their films; they try to use only those sounds recorded more or less synchronously with the images. In several instances, however, the makers of *An American Family* used these techniques. In episode two, after escorting his mother to a taxi, Lance returns to his room at the Chelsea Hotel. Following him in a virtuoso long take, the camera climbs up four flights of stairs and enters his room, where Lance flips on the television in time to catch the end of Abbott and Costello's *Buck Privates Come Home* (1947). "The buck privates have fought their war and won. They march in glory. Their reward? They're going home." The mood of this shot is melancholy, conveyed in some measure by the weary sounds of footsteps fading away in the empty hallways, appropriate enough for the life of a young man from Santa Barbara living alone in New York City.[47]

Unfortunately, no synchronous sound was recorded to accompany this compelling scene. Editor David Hanser returned to the hotel and re-created the echoing sound of footsteps by walking up the stairs, carrying a Nagra recorder, at the same pace as Lance had done. For the sound of the television broadcast, Jacqueline Donnet stated, "We knew exactly the day and the time it was shot and went to the *New York Times* and found out what film it really was, rented the film—and that was the exact same print that they had on the air—and just added it." It is doubtful that any viewer ever noticed this manipulation of the conventions of synchronous sound recording. With the new digital postproduction technologies in use, Donnet admitted that she "wouldn't trust anyone with audio in terms of saying that was really on the track or that wasn't on the track." Short of confessions from the filmmakers, there is no way of knowing for sure whether sound effects were recorded at the time of shooting.

In addition, commentary for *An American Family* was taped at WNET. The production team recorded a voice-over passage by Pat about her parents and her experiences in the 1950s. They also taped Bill Loud reading a letter he had written to Lance explaining his feelings about the separation. Similarly, during the editing, Lance was invited to the studio to re-create his half of a telephone conversation with his mother, recorded before Susan Raymond had installed phone taps. He also improvised some comments about his family that were used in episode one. "When they were editing the show," Lance remembered, "they took me in the recording studio and they had me do overdubs. They just gave me rough outlines of areas they wanted me to talk about." Apart from these instances, the production team maintained a fairly consistent observational approach, so much so that Gilbert would later legitimately claim, "There is more manipulation and staging in one 20-minute segment of *60 Minutes* than there is in all 12 hours of *An American Family*."[48]

Gilbert fought with the new administration of WNET about the form as well as the length of the documentary. The associate producer recalled arguing for maintaining the observational style: "If there was a radical stylistic element to the show, that was it. There were not a lot of documentaries on prime-time television without an on-camera host and voice-over narration." For prime-time TV, an observational nonfiction series was a radical innovation. "Standard documentaries, particularly on network television, take away the discomfort of the real," Lester noted. "They do it by having some anchorperson, someone you already know and you're totally at home with, explain the material. He's going to be there at the beginning, he's going to be there at the end, and it dilutes the material." She maintains that the series has more in common with fiction than with documentary:

> Most nonfiction television comes to the viewer through an intermediary. Shows like *thirtysomething* [1987–91], to me, hearken back more to *An American Family* than most of the documentaries that are on the air. They happen to be telling stories through actors. We were telling a story with real people. But *thirtysomething* feels more like that series than 95 percent of the straight documentaries that are on the air.

The difference between showing and telling—between dramatizing and lecturing—remains one of the central tensions of *An American Family*. Donnet reiterated Lester's claim, "What is so totally different about this series is that no one tells you what to look at and no one tells you what you've seen." Most nonfiction programs on American TV still make extensive use of on-camera hosts, voice-over narration, and interviews. In *Documentary in American Television*, communication scholar A. William Bluem argues against the narrative approach of Drew Associates: "Television journalism can truthfully say, 'This is the way it was' or even 'This is the way it is,' but it is not the function of journalism to say 'This is *it*.'"[49] Pat Loud agreed to appear in the program partly because it used a "non-argumentative" observational style. She later objected to the introductory title graphics because they cued the audience to a particular point of view: "I said I didn't like them breaking us up before we even began, and I felt it was a strong editorial comment."[50]

Gilbert was unable to find outside funds to complete episodes thirteen, fourteen, and fifteen, shows that would have included more scenes of family life after the parents' separation. As a result of the chronological focus, the footage shot in November and December remained, for all practical purposes, on the cutting room floor. Although Hanser could not recall putting together the extra episodes, Donnet insisted that they prepared rough cuts of them. According to the coordinating producer, these programs included considerable material devoted to Mr. Loud. In her view, "Bill Loud comes across like an oaf because you don't see him very much in the early shows. In the missing shows there was more of a concentration on Bill and he turns out to be someone else altogether." Delilah echoed Donnet's perspective in an interview in the *Chicago Tribune:* "I think out of all of us they portrayed my father in the worst light."[51] Just as Pat reminisced in episode four about her childhood and the early years of her marriage, one of the unfinished shows depicted Bill's visit to the battleship *Arizona* in Hawaii and his recollections of World War II.

As per Gilbert's agreement with the family, Pat Loud went to WNET to preview the final versions of the episodes. From Hanser's perspective, this process amounted to little more than a rubber-stamping of the programs: "I felt this was a finished film. In one case, after a particularly painful episode was over, the one leading directly up to their separation, there was just silence in the room. Then she said, 'Well, I guess that's the way it was,' and didn't say anything about deleting anything at all. She just approved it." Speaking on *The Dick Cavett Show,* Lance concurred, "We always got the idea that we couldn't really change anything when we saw it anyway." Only in the case of episode nine did Pat hesitate to approve the final cut. After watching the divorce scene, she said, "I'd let it stand but couldn't speak for Bill. If he passed on it, I would too. So for the first time they sent for Bill. He asked them to take out a couple of lines and they did."[51]

Clearly, the preview deck was stacked in favor of the filmmakers. They were the experts, they understood editing, they understood image and sound juxtapositions, they were *An American Family*'s first audience. Pat had no clue how the program would be received. She could not see her family as television viewers would. She believed Gilbert's perspective that the observational series had no particular point of view, so what was to change in the editing of the episodes? Pat had nothing else to say but her tentative response, "Well, I guess that's the way it was."

Gilbert commissioned Elinor Bunin to prepare a title sequence to open the twelve episodes of *An American Family*.[53] The sequence, which introduces the individual family members, ends with the words "An American Family" shattering like broken glass. The producers did not know how the series would be received and argued among themselves about the title sequence. Because of the intermittent style of television watching, they could not count on viewers' having seen earlier episodes. In addition, they did not anticipate the widespread coverage the program would receive in the media. Donnet felt that the audience needed this reminder—that something was amiss in the family—at the outset of every show. The outpouring of articles about the Louds' separation in the national press eventually made this title sequence embarrassingly redundant.

Gilbert later came to feel that they should not have included the sequence, whereas Donnet believed that it was necessary but that they should have pulled out the shattering frame after episode one. They wanted to give viewers some indication of the thrust of the documentary without having voice-over narration or a host recapitulate the events each week. The coordinating producer noted that the observational approach made this kind of highlighting difficult: "Our very style built in the problem." Donnet wanted viewers to be prepared to search for "the irritations" in the parents' relationship. Lance Loud, for his part, enjoyed the opening graphics. "Nothing seemed more delightfully anarchistic than to be part of this American family that breaks up literally on the screen in the credits."

The form of *An American Family* reflects the producer's point of view. Gilbert chose the family, the crew, the shooting and editing style, the episodic serial narrative, the on-camera introduction, and the title sequence. All along the "lengthy process" of conception, investment, and production, Gilbert straddled artistic and commercial considerations, and tensions between "everyday life" and "great drama." The producer wanted to make an observational series but was not above transgressing that commitment when necessary. Although the style supposedly shows rather than tells the audience what to think, Gilbert hesitated to leave viewers entirely on their own. He added additional signposts, giving the lie to the idea that the documentary puts forward no particular point of view.

Station president James Day saw the completed episodes for the first time at a prescreening in Los Angeles in late December 1972. "It was simply part of my style of management," Day recalled, "not to demand to see things that were works in progress. I had complete confidence in the people who worked for me." The broadcast of episode one was scheduled for January 11, 1973. The production team worked feverishly—the editors went into triple overtime pay—to complete the series on time. When the broadcast started, they were still editing the later shows. WNET sponsored a private premiere in early January at the Slate, a restaurant at 56th Street and 10th Avenue, a favorite of Gilbert. A large television set mounted in the restaurant showed several episodes. The audience, composed mainly of staff and crew, applauded the names that appeared in the credits and celebrated with food and drink. "We really felt a sense of accomplishment," Carey recalled.

By the time they were putting the finishing touches on the early shows, Hanser and the others gradually realized, based on sneak previews held at the station, that the documentary was going to have a big impact. Journalists from *Life* came more than once to view the work in progress.

At the first official press screening at the Museum of Modern Art, WNET distributed a packet of materials that included a copy of an article from *Image,* the in-house magazine of Channel 13. On the cover of the magazine was a drawing based on an old Christmas card photo of the Loud family, "all black and spidery and burned-looking at the bottom," as Pat later recalled, "with cracks going up and separating us all from one another."[54] As it turned out, this was just the beginning of a slew of negative publicity about the Louds and highly critical reviews of *An American Family.*

The cover of WNET's membership magazine *Image.*

II A Closer Look at
An American Family

[3] "A Bastard Union of Several Forms"

> *Our story begins in the Loud home at 35 Wooddale Lane. . . .*
> :: Craig Gilbert, episode one

If the emphasis on intimate family life was rare for a documentary at the time, so was the observational style of *An American Family*. The series presents an unfolding story, using principles of Western drama routinely applied in classical Hollywood cinema and dramatic television. Documentaries are often mistakenly classified as nonnarrative films, but narrative is a story of events and experiences *either* fictitious or true. Many, although not all, documentaries tell stories. *An American Family* certainly does. Events in the series flow along a chain of cause and effect as well as sequence. Within individual scenes, the setting, the characters, the time, and the action are usually clearly identifiable. In episode three, for example, Delilah's preparations for her dance recital culminate in a public performance with her parents in attendance.

Narrative omniscience remains the order of the day; the story is not restricted to one character's point of view, but roams freely. Coverage of the annual recital of the Rudenko School of Dance—an evening's entertainment condensed into less than ten minutes of screen time—presents sequential and simultaneous actions occurring backstage, onstage, and in the audience, shown from a panoply of different angles. Numerous performances by Delilah and Michele are featured. Music bridges the movement from the stage to the dressing room, maintaining continuous spatial and temporal relations, just as the strains of *Swan Lake* announce the transition back to the stage. This sequence, and the episode with it, ends with a freeze frame of Bill and Pat Loud applauding from their seats in the Lobero Theater in Santa Barbara. Throughout, *An American Family* combines the shooting style of observational cinema with particular features of television as a storytelling medium. In this chapter, I offer a survey of the development and evolution of the observational style during the decades after World War II, before returning to consider the innovative multiple-focus narrative structure of Gilbert's series.

▶

The Observational Style

In the 1950s, innovators in television journalism applied different principles of storytelling to the nonfiction format in an attempt to move away from illustrated lectures. Following the example of the photojournalism of *Life* magazine, producers such as Robert Drew wanted to give the impression of lived experience by recording events on location as they happened. During a Nieman Fellowship at Harvard in 1954, Drew studied the structure of the nineteenth-century realist short story, a form he wanted to apply to documentary. In particular, Drew was fascinated by narrative voice in the writings of nineteenth-century novelist Gustave Flaubert, works in which the story seems to tell itself.[1] Returning to New York with funding from Time-Life to create a new kind of actuality film, Drew assembled a team of talented young filmmakers to form Drew Associates: Richard Leacock, D. A. Pennebaker, Albert and David Maysles, Hope Ryden, James Lipscomb, Gregory Shuker, and others.

These filmmakers wanted to eliminate overt devices of narration, such as voice-over, in favor of stories that begin in medias res and unfold seemingly without a narrator. Drew believed that film and television are essentially visual media, and he hoped to avoid word-driven approaches to documentary, approaches that relied on interviews, voice-over narration, and on-camera hosts. Drew Associates opted for found stories that had inherent drama with clear beginnings, middles, and ends. Their films, like Hollywood movies, were typically structured around strong protagonists during moments of crisis.[2] French critics were quick to note the classicism of Drew's documentaries, comparing them to the films of Howard Hawks.[3]

In the 1960s, observational filmmakers such as Robert Drew may have claimed that their narrative style was more faithful to reality, but the classical Hollywood cinema, whose roots may also be found in nineteenth-century realism, also provided a clear example for the new documentary. As documentarist David MacDougall has stated, "Many of us who began applying an observational approach to ethnographic filmmaking found ourselves taking as our model not the documentary film as we had come to know it since Grierson, but the dramatic fiction film, in all its incarnations from Tokyo to Hollywood."[4] Arguing that they were brushing up against the truth, however, nonfiction producers could hardly cite American fictional cinema as their model; this was a period when many independent filmmakers defined Hollywood as their enemy. In 1983, however, Drew admitted, "You don't need Dan Rather in the middle of a fiction motion picture to tell you what's going on."[5]

These directors abandoned the established Griersonian tradition of direct address—best known for the ubiquitous "voice of God" spoken narration—in favor of a style that used techniques of storytelling and continuity editing conventionally associated with fiction films. All forms of explicit address to the viewer were to be avoided in favor of an impersonal narration similar to classical Hollywood cinema. The push toward an observational style in documentary contributed to the breakdown of strict divisions between fiction and nonfiction in the 1960s. As documentary filmmakers embraced storytelling, feature filmmakers such as French new wave director Jean-Luc Godard experimented with location-recorded sound, shooting with available light, improvisation, interviews, and voice-over narration.

At Drew Associates in the late 1950s, Drew, Leacock, and Pennebaker, together with the Maysles brothers, consciously worked to revolutionize the documentary form. They hated "illustrated lectures," such as *Victory at Sea,* on which Craig Gilbert had worked as an assistant film editor. "It was just stock shots," Pennebaker recalled, with voice-over commentary by Leonard Graves, who had a "terrible, very English accent." Using shots patched together from a variety of sources and battles, and wall-to-wall music composed by Richard Rodgers, *Victory at Sea* gave Pennebaker the strange impression "that there was no war at all."[6] Conventions of realism were changing; Pennebaker's principal interest as a filmmaker was not in lecturing viewers, but in capturing the mood and feel of everyday life.

Like Pennebaker, Robert Drew wanted to convey a sense of "being there" through film. Trained as a journalist for *Life* magazine, but strongly influenced by fiction film and the realist novel, he cited the differences between showing and telling. "Most documentary films were in fact lectures. They were then, and most remain today, lectures with picture illustrations. It was as clear as the lectures I was attending every day at Harvard and thrown into relief by the novels and plays I was reading every night."[7] By recording events when they happened, Drew sought to bring "picture logic"—that is, character, narrative, and continuity editing—to documentary, as opposed to the "word logic" of on-camera commentary, voice-over narration, and interviews.

Leacock expressed an even more radical position vis-à-vis nonfiction television. A combat cinematographer during World War II, he worked with

Robert Flaherty, the quintessential independent director, on *Louisiana Story* (1948). The young apprentice took the works of Flaherty and the Italian neorealists as models for his own. He and Pennebaker quit Drew Associates because they felt that Drew was in the business of making documentaries "appetizing for television," as Pennebaker put it.[8] Leacock eventually turned his back on public as well as commercial TV, becoming a staunch supporter of low-budget independent cinema.[9]

In the mid-1960s, modernist variations on the narrative style of observational cinema quickly emerged in the independent documentary community. The Maysles brothers constructed open-ended episodic narratives in *Showman* (1962) and *What's Happening! The Beatles in the U.S.A.* (1964) while Andy Warhol explored minimalist experiments in *Sleep* (1963) and *Empire* (1964). In works like *Salesman* (1969), a portrait of door-to-door Bible salesmen on the road in Florida, the Maysleses moved toward neorealist screenwriter Cesare Zavattini's call for a film that portrayed ninety minutes in the life of an ordinary man. Warhol, in his early works, drained the observational style of any interest in narrative, emphasizing time over plot. For example, *Sleep*, which lasts five hours and twenty-one minutes, features nothing other than the sleeping and snoring body of performer John Giorno. Jim McBride and L. M. Kit Carson parodied the search for

The top of the Empire State Building from Andy Warhol's eight-hour tour de force *Empire* (1964).

truth in their mock autobiography *David Holzman's Diary* (1967), and
Allan King looked at private life in *A Married Couple* (1969). Wiseman,
eschewing the earlier concentration on personalities as subjects, introduced
a multiple-focus narrative structure for his early films on everyday life in
American social institutions: *High School* (1969), *Law and Order* (1969),
and *Hospital* (1970). *An American Family,* a twelve-hour observational
portrait of intimate family life, represents a compromise among these different tendencies, bridging the stylistic conventions of independent documentary film and broadcast TV. Gilbert adapted the innovations of American cinema verité to the traditions of television.

As a style, observational cinema tends more toward the spontaneous
and improvised approach of Italian neorealist Roberto Rossellini than to
the scripted and densely plotted work of Alfred Hitchcock or Alain Resnais.
Vis-à-vis traditional documentaries, observational films are open to multiple
interpretations; they lack the devices of voice-over, interviews, and scored
music through which point of view may be unequivocally expressed. An
open work that struggles with its own formative tendencies, *An American
Family* ends on a decisively ambiguous note. Discussing her likely alimony
arrangement, Pat Loud mentions that she may never marry again. Her dinner guest remarks, "I find this the most depressing conversation I've ever
heard in my bloody life." Pat replies, "But these things happen," and the

A teacher and students in Wiseman's *High School.*

final episode freezes on her smiling face. Despite the narrative continuity of many parts of the series, there is no neat resolution.

▶
Serial and Multiple-Focus Narrative

An American Family capitalizes on one of the dominant historical characteristics of American television, namely, serial narrative. Scene changes are facilitated by the large cast of principal characters and the ability to shift the focus of the narrative from one family member to another. Story lines developed at one point are temporarily abandoned only to be picked up later. This multiple-focus narrative results in several ongoing plotlines. For example, Grant's band practices in the garage in episode one, discusses music contracts in hour three, performs at a high school pep rally in episode ten, and auditions for a club gig in the final program. Episode two, on the other hand, showcases Lance's life at the Chelsea Hotel when Pat arrives for a weeklong visit to New York. *An American Family* presents not the linear causal chain of classical Hollywood cinema, with its goal-oriented protagonists, but rather the slow pace of serial narrative, confirming media critic John Ellis's intuition that, on television, "The normal movement between segments is one of vague simultaneity (meanwhile . . . meanwhile . . . a bit later . . .)."[10]

In *Speaking of Soap Operas,* film and TV scholar Robert Allen describes the characteristics that distinguish daytime serials from other narrative forms: a continuous format that draws out stories indefinitely, multiple characters and multiple narrative plotlines, and a focus on the intimate daily lives of the characters.[11] Soaps rely on consistent viewer involvement over weeks, months, and years; the entire background and personality of a particular character will be relevant to that person's actions. *An American Family* shares these characteristics, including an emphasis on character over plot. Many of the scenes simply give insight into the family members and their relationships without advancing any story lines, so that Pat's visit to her mother in episode four focuses on the women's shared history, not on any future event. (In fact, in terms of narrative development, Mrs. Loud's trip to Eugene *delays* the main plotline of her deteriorating relationship with her husband.) As such, the program contributes to the cross-fertilization of genre in contemporary American television. Although some critics credit *Dallas* as "the beginning of a new genre in American TV, combining the afternoon soap with other prime-time forms," this stylistic innovation clearly appeared in Gilbert's 1973 series.[12]

Episodic story structure employs greater redundancy than classical

Hollywood narrative. Daytime television serials reiterate plot developments extensively to keep irregular viewers up to date. In *An American Family,* although most scenes occur only once, there are interesting exceptions. In hour eight, having returned from a trip to mining companies across the country, Bill asks his son Grant, "How's everything on the home front?" Mr. Loud anticipates trouble at home: "Walking right into the lion's den, huh?" The episode then ends with a freeze frame of father and son set off against the darkness of the Santa Barbara airport; jet engines roar ominously in the distance as the credits roll over their frozen expressions. Like a flashback that recaps earlier story events, hour nine opens with Mr. Loud's arrival at the airport as Gilbert reiterates the situation in voice-over: "It is the evening of September 3rd. Grant is driving to the airport to pick up his father, who is returning to Santa Barbara after a three-week business trip." The show then repeats the inauspicious exchange between Bill and Grant in its entirety. While filling in background, the repetition also signals its importance, further building suspense for Bill's return to 35 Wooddale Lane and the encounter in which his wife will ask him to move out.

■——

Multiple Characters

Like most multiple-focus narrative television shows—especially soap operas—*An American Family* offers viewers choices for sympathetic identification with different characters, their values, and behaviors. Most consistently, the series contrasts Mr. and Mrs. Loud's conflicting attitudes toward marriage and parenting, implicitly suggesting a "battle of the sexes" drama typical of television situation comedies. Unlike in sitcoms, however, this battle is treated without humor and easy resolution. Dining out in episode six, Pat expresses concern about their children leaving home. Bill replies, "Life's too short to worry about all that jazz." She counters, "I hate to see them go like that. I hate it." The series ends with a scene of Bill at lunch with a friend talking about marriage and its discontents, followed by a parallel scene of Pat at dinner with friends discussing her likely divorce settlement.

On the basis of time devoted to her, Pat emerges as the lead character in the series. Mrs. Loud's attitude evolves toward her role as wife and mother. At the beginning of episode three, after she inspects a shipment of materials in Baltimore for her husband's business, the company representative gives her a backhanded compliment: "Well, I think that you did a very good job for a housewife." Over the course of the series, Pat gradually

Bill and Pat Loud dine out in *An American Family.*

changes from a married homemaker to a single mother looking for work. Episode four focuses almost exclusively on Pat, her personal and family history, and her relationship with her mother. It details her memories through exceptional techniques, such as first-person voice-over narration, home movies, and snapshots. Five subjective flashbacks introduce incidents in Pat's childhood and young adult years. As she peers into her old house in Eugene, stating, "I loved that fireplace," the program cuts to a point-of-view zoom into an old photograph of her children sitting in front of it. Even so, the narration remains mostly omniscient for this nostalgic journey home. While Mrs. Loud eats lunch during her flight, the documentary cuts to a panorama of the city of Eugene, only to return to Pat on the plane in the following shot.

The family members represent different normative systems: the work ethic of Bill and to a lesser extent Pat, the pleasure principle of the children (especially Grant), and the avant-garde, *épater le bourgeois* attitude of Lance. In episode three, Bill complains to Pat at lunch about the boys, "They're lazy, God, they're lazy." Although occasionally blatantly articulated, contrasts often remain implicit within the program. Having seen *Vain Victory,* the drag queen parody of the American musical at La Mama Theater in Greenwich Village, in hour two, viewers cannot avoid comparisons with the amateur dance performances of Delilah and Michele in the following episode at the annual recital of the Rudenko School of Dance in Santa Barbara. Although the sequencing favors the transvestites, which of the performers look ridiculous also depends on the attitudes of audience members.

An independent businessman, Bill Loud embodies a conservative entrepreneurial mentality that his children, and the series itself, ridicule. For example, episode five contrasts the main characters' attitudes toward work. Bill organizes a trip abroad for his second son, which Gilbert describes in voice-over: "Kevin and Glen Volkenaught, Bill's top salesman, will be leaving to visit mines and explore new business opportunities in Australia and Southeast Asia." The subject of the American war in Vietnam remains beneath the surface; no one directly addresses the implications of the fight to preserve capitalism in Asia. Later, urging his eighteen-year-old son to take advantage of this opportunity to meet people abroad, Bill remarks, "They'll be glad to see you, Kevin. God, they're glad to see Americans when they get over there." Similarly, in episode eleven, Mr. Loud invites Lance to accompany him with Kevin to "see the bombers come in." Lance politely declines.

Bill also wants to find work for his other son still living at home. Unaware of his father's plans, Grant listens to the Who sing "Won't Get Fooled Again" on his record player; hinting at utopian desires unfulfilled, Roger Daltrey exhorts his young admirer to "take a bow for the new revolution." Mr. Loud, on the other hand, hopes to get his languid third son to work in construction, during his summer vacation, for the "curb king of Southern California." He talks to his nephew about summer employment for Grant, even volunteering to pay his son's wages. Offered a job pouring cement, the seventeen-year-old shows little interest in the prospect of physical labor, referring to his father's machinations as "the concrete caper."

Subsequently, at the airport, Mr. Loud, Kevin, and Glen discuss the pleasures of work. Bill describes the beauty of strip-mining: "When that great big Marion 5600 shovel throws that bucket out there and sucks that dirt back up there, and it's cold, you know, and you see more metal roll off that thing, I mean, you're on Broadway, you know. You're really at the top of the heap." The program then follows Bill's euphoric remarks with a scene of Grant at work on a hot summer day; he's definitely not on Broadway. Although the sun has set during their ride to the airport, the episode cuts to a daytime sequence of Grant and then back to Kevin at the departure gate, a clear manipulation of story order to contrast the two perspectives.

Episode seven picks up this comparison, and argument between the generations, as Grant complains to his dad about a lack of support for his career interests in music: "I'm not even going to go into it with you, because you'll just give me all this jazz about, well, 'You gotta go to college and take some economics, and a banking course, and you'll be set for the rest of your life.'" Laughing, Bill remains true to form in his response, "Well, don't you think you would be?" In episode eight, Mr. Loud jokingly tells some mine workers that his son Grant is "the forerunner of the three-day week." For his part, Lance, traveling abroad in hour six, invents a story about having his money stolen so that his parents will send more. In the final show, Bill refers to his eldest son as the "greatest con artist you ever saw." Through these juxtapositions, viewers of *An American Family* have the opportunity to identify with different family members according to their interests. The multiple-focus narrative style leaves room for audiences "to root for" their favorite Loud, as literary critic Roger Rosenblatt pointed out in the *New Republic*.[13]

The documentary itself frequently favors Lance's perspective for the critique he extends of his family and life in general in Southern California. Only Lance and Pat have individual episodes devoted to them. Purchasing a ticket at Kennedy International Airport for his return to the West Coast in episode eleven, Lance tells the reservations clerk that Santa Barbara is "more than just a home, it's a way of life." The program, however, does not limit itself to Lance's bohemian point of view. Editorial perspective circulates freely among the different characters. In the final hour, Mr. Loud's

Pat and Lance Loud in Central Park in *An American Family*.

friend Robert sums up the pessimistic point of view of *An American Family* during a lunch date with Bill: "The family as we knew it in our youth is a thing of the past and you see all the signs of it coming to an end."

In addition to these dialogue exchanges, transitions between scenes remain pivotal moments for editorial commentary. In episode eight, Pat summarizes her feelings about marriage for her brother and sister-in-law: "It was my life and it didn't work." The show then cuts to a close-up of the jaws of a strip-mining shovel and the roar of a crane. "I want you to notice how very sharp those teeth are," Bill says admiringly. Later, riding through the mine fields, Mr. Loud mentions his wife's recent trip to Taos and the jewelry she purchased there, adding, "Beauty is in the eye of the beholder," a comment that continues over a shot of Pat in the kitchen at 35 Wooddale Lane. These devices, and others, become apparent in the detailed analysis of a single episode presented in the next chapter.

[4] Opening Night: Episode One

Episode one is the most didactic of all the shows, making use of a flash-back structure, parallel editing, on-camera narration, and a general "day in the life" approach rather than the basic chronology of the rest of the series. Later shows have looser narrative structures and more diffuse editorial stances. The first hour introduces the family members, their individual and common interests, while simultaneously instructing viewers how to look at and understand this unusual documentary. Not counting the title sequence, there are approximately twenty-four scenes and 169 shots. A typical scene here is two-and-a-half minutes long, composed of seven shots of an average length of twenty-one seconds each. However, within this general framework, there is considerable variety. A scene of the Loud family at breakfast lasts seven and a half minutes and consists of thirty-four shots, whereas Delilah's dance rehearsal lasts several minutes but consists of just one elegant long take.

After a prologue introduction by Craig Gilbert and the title sequence, the next twelve scenes take place on December 31, which the voice-over refers to as "the last day of filming." Preparations for the 1971 New Year's celebration and the party itself are condensed into thirty minutes of film. Most of these activities take place at "35 Wooddale Lane," although Bill Loud appears in new lodgings at the Park Cabrillo Apartments. Later, the program cuts between the party at the Louds' home and Bill's celebration at the Somerset nightclub with his new girlfriend, Linda. Scenes fifteen through twenty-five then take place "seven months earlier." After breakfast with the entire family, the documentary showcases the separate activities of the Louds during a "typical" day. These vignettes come from different moments over the seven-month shooting schedule: Delilah's dance recital occurred in June, Bill's tour of mining operations took place in August, and Grant's class at Santa Barbara High School met in the fall.

The Prologue and Signature Montage

The series opens with a short on-camera prologue delivered by Craig Gilbert. He evidently felt that the experimental nature of the program required some explanation. He speaks directly to the camera: "During the next hour, you will see the first in a series of programs entitled *An American Family*. The series is about the William C. Loud family, of Santa Barbara, California." Gilbert's opening monologue, in which he attempts to frame audience expectations and deflect possible criticisms, stands apart from the observational model. Contradicting the thrust of the series title, he contends that the Louds are "neither average nor typical, no family is. They are not the American family, they are simply an American family." Clearly, however, the Louds were intended to stand for American families in general. Other comments in the prologue make ample use of tropes of representativeness to describe the Louds, including such qualifying statements as "like all families," "like most of us," and "like their parents before them."

The title implies a certain level of generality, which may be compared to Wiseman's series of generic titles for his films, including *High School, Hospital, Basic Training, Juvenile Court, Welfare,* and *Model.* Wiseman encourages viewers to think of the institutions shown as abstract examples, not particular instances. Gilbert could have called his series *The Loud Family of Santa Barbara, California.* In fact, the next American non-fiction television series on family life, *Six American Families* (1976), followed just this strategy, with individual episodes titled "The Burks of Georgia," "The Pasciaks of Chicago," "The Stephens of Iowa," "The Georges of New York," "The Kennedys of Albuquerque," and "The Greenbergs of California."

Gilbert's introduction addresses a host of important questions about typicality, ethics, and objectivity that remain submerged throughout the main body of the twelve-hour documentary. In his prologue, he admits that the presence of the filmmakers inevitably affected the Louds, an influence that "is impossible to evaluate." The producer asks viewers to recognize certain rules of the game, that the Louds behaved "as if" the camera were not there and, correspondingly, that viewers, too, should watch the series "as if" the camera were not there. Gilbert asserts that the program was a cooperative venture "in every sense of the word," although few traces of this interaction appear in the series itself. The tensions of the observational approach—between showing and telling, between the particular and the general, between recording and creating—are transferred to the opening monologue. A similar displacement occurs in John Huston's *The Battle of San Pietro* (1945), in which an introductory statement from a representative of the army attempts to deflect the main point of view of the film. Gilbert's prologue is a perfect instance of stylistic conflict in *An American Family*.

The producer continues his description of the setting of the series: "The population of Santa Barbara is somewhere around 73,000. Located on a slope of the Santa Ynez Mountains, Santa Barbara faces south on the Pacific Ocean, ninety miles north of Los Angeles—driving time an hour and a half, flying time twenty minutes. The average daytime temperature is 78 degrees in summer and 65 degrees in winter." This description establishes the city as nothing less than idyllic, a suburban paradise framed by mountains and ocean. Throughout this introduction, Gilbert sounds curiously like the Stage Manager in Thornton Wilder's *Our Town* (1938), who sets the stage for a reenactment of family life both particular and universal. Like the Stage Manager, Gilbert remains somewhat detached from the everyday affairs of ordinary mortals. After introducing the characters and the setting, he disappears. Indeed, *Our Town* presents a model for understanding *An American Family* as social commentary; both make appeals to family, community, and nation. The camera and tape recorder serve as witnesses to the events, an internal audience like Emily, who returns, after her death, to observe the living going about their everyday lives.

In both *Our Town* and *An American Family*, viewers are invited to see "Daily Life" with its ordinary significance heightened. Because the documentary opens with the last day of filming and the voice-over narration gives away the drama of the program immediately, viewers look for signs of a troubled marriage. At the moment Pat first appears, Gilbert states, "This New Year's will be unlike any other that has been celebrated at 35 Wooddale Lane. For the first time the family will not be spending it together. Pat Loud and her husband, Bill, separated four months ago after twenty years of marriage." As in Greek drama and popular film genres, we know the end already, and the suspense lies more in the telling than in the tale. Like the Stage Manager of *Our Town*, Gilbert embodies the "voice of God," knowing the end and the beginning. Throughout the rest of the twelve-hour series, he resurfaces sporadically to provide the time and place of the action.

Thanks to this teleological structure, viewers know the outcome of *An American Family* from the opening episode. The flashback form compounds the already disturbing association of the observational style with voyeurism, the opportunity for viewers to observe people without being observed. The narration provides information about the future to which the characters do not have access. When the Louds sat down for breakfast in May 1971, they did not know that in September Pat would file for divorce and Bill would move into a downtown apartment. In this way, viewers know more than the Louds do. This hierarchy of knowledge may have contributed to the smugness apparent in many reviewers' comments on the family.

Despite the central emphasis placed here on the Louds' separation, their marriage only indirectly surfaces as an issue in the next five hours of *An American Family*. Bill does not appear at all during episode two; in hour four, he figures in only one scene, on the telephone with Lance. Indirect references to marital problems in the early shows become comprehensible to the viewer only in light of Gilbert's announcement that they have separated. The state of their relationship must be inferred on the basis of its relative *absence* in the narrative; for example, Pat and Bill take separate vacations in episodes four and five. As a result, the central dilemma of the documentary remains tantalizingly off-screen for much of the series, indefinitely postponed through story techniques that delay the eventual separation until episode nine.

After the prologue and at the outset of each subsequent episode, a split-screen montage title sequence and musical theme song introduce the family members one by one: Pat and then Bill, and the children in descending order of age, Lance, Kevin, Grant, Delilah, Michele. The title montage looks and sounds a lot like the openings to *The Brady Bunch* (1969–74) and *The Partridge Family* (1970–74). An upbeat musical jingle accompanies the images of family members going about activities seen in the body of the series; Bill visits a strip-mining field, Pat speaks on the phone, Michele grooms her pet horse, and so on. A freeze frame isolates each of the Louds in a separate space on the screen. The title *An American Family*, white on red, superimposes on the boxed images of the family members. In a musical crescendo, the title breaks up explosively, announcing the split of the family.

Nothing in Gilbert's series smacks of television situation comedies so much as this title sequence. As British TV scholar John Ellis argues: "The title sequence is in effect a commercial for the programme itself, and it has all the features of a commercial. It is considerably more expensive per second than the programme it fronts; it is highly organised and synoptic, providing a kind of narrative image for its programme."[1] Even more than the episodic structure, the suburban setting, and the family focus, the signature montage calls to mind other television representations of family life. Given these associations, *An American Family* needed to be in color, because black-and-white film would have tagged the show as an educational documentary. The musical introduction, composed specifically for the opening montage, serves as the theme song of *An American Family,* a signature refrain for the program like those that open situation comedies such as *One Day at a Time* (1975–84). At the outset of every episode, it reintroduces the characters and reiterates the central narrative dilemma. In this passage, Gilbert conforms to the standards and conventions of broadcast television, rather than independent film, a balancing act that becomes more apparent over the course of the documentary.

▶━━━

In My End Is My Beginning

After the opening montage, the first scene begins with the Louds' preparations for the 1971 New Year's Day party in their home. While these events take place, Bill Loud, alone in his apartment, opens Christmas cards. As Gilbert's voice-over announces that Bill spent his holiday vacation in Hawaii, the viewer encounters Mr. Loud for the first time. He mechanically sifts through a large pile of Christmas cards, chuckling laconically in response to one of them. (Later in this episode, after the story shifts back to the month of May, Pat suggests to Lance that he send his dad a Hallmark card for Father's Day, even though she finds them "silly.") The parallel editing structure implies simultaneity of time and indeed, later, the program cuts back and forth between Bill in his singles apartment and Pat at home. They have a terse exchange on the phone about his Hawaiian getaway. Another phone conversation, between the Louds' fifteen-year-old daughter, Delilah, and her boyfriend, Brad, immediately follows this exchange. Their awkward tenderness contrasts vividly with the tired cynicism of her parents. The poignant symbolism of the New Year, with its retrospective glance toward the past and resolutions for the future, underlines the entire sequence.

Pat is the only adult present at the festivities at 35 Wooddale Lane. The camera lingers on her isolation and apparent loneliness as she reads, pets the dog, and watches her children dance to the Andrews Sisters singing "Boogie Woogie Bugle Boy." Strictly parallel scenes compare her evening to Bill's. (Sound advances anticipating the next scene frequently bridge transitions between sequences. Slow dissolves serve the same function here.) A close-up on Pat's face dissolves to a shot of Bill dancing with another woman, suggesting the source of Pat's discontent. The strains of Carole King's "You've Got a Friend," sung by a piano man in the background, fill in the details. Later that evening, as he celebrates with friends, Mr. Loud tells an anecdote about his recent car accident. "You wake up,"

Bill recalls, "and you realize that you've been in a wonderful wreck," a comment that, given the context, suggests a carefree attitude toward his separation as well.

When the story of the Louds jumps back to late spring, the future hangs heavy over the present. (Having shown the effects—the Louds' separation—the episode returns to explore the causes. The flashback structure strongly encourages a cause-and-effect chain of associations.) Pat's irritation as she prepares breakfast plays as her dissatisfaction with her lot. Bill appears and asks if she has seen his shoes. "No sir," she replies curtly, "I'll look for them." During a lawn party later, Bill inquires if another woman plans to stay long in Santa Barbara. Suspicious, Pat asks why. As her husband pleads innocent curiosity, Pat remarks, "Well for the record, she's just passing through," provoking laughter from the group. The camera lingers on Bill's nervous chuckle, hinting at his affairs and Pat's growing anger. The seeds of the coming discord ripen in these exchanges. This atmosphere of marital infidelity, once established, pervades the documentary. In episode six, the Louds notice some acquaintances at a restaurant. "Gee, he's with his wife today," Pat says, feigning astonishment, while Bill adds, "There goes Mr. . . . with his scintillating companion of the evening."

Having raised the marital question during the "late spring morning," the first episode cuts three thousand miles to New York City to introduce the one family member not present at the breakfast meal. When Lance speaks for the first time, he delivers a long tirade entirely in voice-over about his family, while sorting his clothes in a room at the Chelsea Hotel. He describes his siblings in a sort of interior monologue: "I have two brothers and two sisters; Kevin, Grant, Delilah, and Michele. I don't know any of their ages or any of their birthdays or anything like that. I can never remember anything of those private things of anybody, except my own." Although he has yet to find work in Manhattan, Lance rejects the idea of returning to the West Coast to "get a little job and make everybody happy."

This scene provides a forum for Lance to introduce his siblings and underlines his status as an outsider; he has escaped the easy life of the Santa Barbara upper middle class. No other member of the family provides this kind of commentary on the others. Lance describes Kevin as "torn between so many worlds. He wants to be hip but Dad wants him to be, you know, the image of his own self"; Delilah is "becoming aware of human relations." The shots of Lance arranging his clothes reveal little, but his voice-over reflections demonstrate wit, insight, narcissism, and a critical distance from home. "Michele," he continues, "of all my brothers and sisters, she's the only one that was made in the image of me. Thank God. I thought that they'd all just go away and I'd be forgotten like a Fizzie or something. But she's becoming selfish and snotty and oh, she's just really a great person." Finally, Grant comes under fire: "He's the most arrogant and hard to get along with. Not a lack of feeling toward other people. He doesn't like other people. He's really funny when he's nice though." This passage—a stylistic rupture in the flow of synchronous images and sounds—endorses Lance's point of view. It ends with his perception of his seventeen-year-old brother: "I think that of all of us Grant will probably succeed most, unfortunately."

Although the multiple-focus narrative allows for abrupt shifts from story line to story line, or character to character, a degree of continuity carries one sequence into another. For example, Lance's comment that his brother Grant "will probably succeed most" sets up the next scene. In a social studies class at Santa Barbara High School, Grant gives a report on the Reconstruction period in American history. His teacher tries to get him to elaborate on his description of the period as a "tragic era." Grant's lackluster performance in class amusingly contradicts Lance's prediction. A medium close-up of Grant holds for a long time as he struggles to find a suitable response; the justification for such a long take comes at the end. After much clowning for the class, Grant remarks that Reconstruction was an attempt to give blacks "equal social status with the whites," so that they,

Grant Loud in class at Santa Barbara High in *An American Family.*

too, could achieve "the American dream." The rationale for the scene no longer concerns Grant's ability; rather, it concerns the rich associations suggested by his remark about race and class in American society.

The following shot shows Mrs. Loud pushing an overflowing shopping cart at a supermarket; she can barely squeeze in another bottle of salad dressing. Purchasing goods for a family of seven, Pat clearly has no time for comparison shopping. Grant's reference to the "American dream" carries over as a commentary on the family's upper-middle-class way of life, consisting of taken-for-granted material abundance. The combination of these two shots gives rise to a concept not inherent in the individual images. The cut provides the series' most blatant example of what Russian documentary filmmaker Esther Shub called "the power of scissors and cement in relation to meaning."[2] The reference to "the American dream," a crucial one for the program, stands out due to a heavy-handed juxtaposition of otherwise unrelated scenes.

In the next sequence, viewers learn where the money comes from that supports the family's comfortable lifestyle. Mr. Loud stands beneath an enormous forklift in a strip-mining field. As he discusses the sale of industrial tools with another man in a hard hat, they watch a hill in the distance explode. "Gee," Bill notes, "that's beautiful," an ironic comment on

Pat Loud shopping for groceries in *An American Family*.

commonsense notions of natural splendor. Only someone who profits from strip-mining could see the blast in that light. Having provided a glimpse of Bill at work, the episode cuts to Delilah and her class rehearsing a dance routine to "In the Mood." There is an awkward adolescent grace to their steps, which the camera catches in a long take. The program continues to introduce the Louds during a typical day and sets up future story actions, such as Delilah's dance recital in episode three and Bill's trip to mining operations in episode eight.

Delilah's segment segues into an afternoon cocktail party, an event that includes Bill and that would have been difficult to cut to directly from his scene in the mining field. The cocktail party comes closest to capturing the mood of the detective novels of Ross Macdonald, which Gilbert and Alan Raymond acknowledged as an influence on their work. The careless party chatter, the sunglasses, the liquor, the leathered faces, the Hawaiian shirts, and the suggestion of extramarital affairs all combine to create an atmosphere of upper-middle-class suburban decadence, California-style. (In episode five, Pat jokes with friends in Taos about her adopted state: "The theory is that all of California is like Sodom and Gomorrah; it's all going to drop into the sea—God's wrath and all.") The cocktail party sequence ends on Pat's repartee to Bill's query about another woman. In the next sequence, Michele grooms her horse, a gentle moment all the more tranquil for coming after the noisy party. In addition to demonstrating her love of animals, it shows the family's wealth, which allows her to pursue such a costly hobby.

Michele's peaceful horse ride through the Santa Barbara hills shatters with a transition to a raucous rehearsal of "Jumpin' Jack Flash" by Kevin and Grant's garage band. The music provides another long-take sequence of entertaining spectacle as the camera sways in tandem with the players. Meanwhile, in the living room, Pat, Bill, Delilah, and Michele take turns talking to Lance on the telephone. The long-distance phone call, like the band's substantial equipment, signals a level of considerable affluence. A rousing performance of "Summertime Blues" ends episode one and leads into the credit sequence. Like the dancers at Delilah's rehearsal, the band performs perfectly routine versions of the songs, held together primarily by the musicians' evident enthusiasm and good humor.

The relationships among the linked sequences of episode one consist of the "vague simultaneity" that Ellis notes of television narration in general.[3] As the family finishes breakfast and starts a new day, Lance sorts his clothes at the Chelsea Hotel. Later, Grant answers questions in class. With the kids at school, Pat shops. While his wife takes care of the home, Bill

Kevin Loud plays the bass in *An American Family.*

works in the field. (Bit by bit, time passes.) After school, Delilah practices her dance routine. After a day of hard work done, Bill and Pat enjoy cocktails with friends, while Michele prefers a quiet ride on horseback. Kevin and Grant, for their part, play rock music. As the band rehearses, the others converse with Lance on the phone. By the evening, the end of a "typical day," the family has come together. A final rowdy version of "Summertime Blues" caps off the show. A freeze frame of the band closes the episode, and the credits roll. Although the underlying organization of the episode is quite sophisticated for a documentary, the impression of the casual unfolding of daily life prevails in the first sixty minutes of *An American Family.*

▶

Breakfast with the Louds

Thirty minutes into episode one, the Loud family prepares breakfast as the voice-over briefly states, "Our story begins seven months earlier, at six-thirty on a late spring morning." The following scene fulfills the stated goals of observational cinema inasmuch as there are no interviews, scored music, or voice-over narration. Similarly, the family members never address the camera. As in fictional television, the viewer intuits the underlying drama and significance of the action by watching the characters and listening to their words. The scene displays a fluid unity of time, space, action, and character.

The breakfast provides a host of information about the Louds. Pat and her daughters are the only family members working in the kitchen, suggesting a traditional division of labor in the home. The tone of Mrs. Loud's voice and the terseness of her comments suggest repressed discontent. Over the course of the twelve episodes, Pat's anger grows and bursts into view, culminating in her demand for a divorce. Mr. Loud, on the other hand, avoids direct conflict in this scene and chooses instead to joke with his kids about their neglect of the backyard. Bill's jocular attitude, even in the face of adversity, remains his most engaging personality trait in the program. When Kevin asks for lunch money, Mr. Loud complains about his laziness. Bill's grumbling about the lack of a work ethic becomes a constant refrain. During breakfast, both parents try to reason with their children rather than give orders, a pattern that continues throughout the series. (The final episode shows a "family conference" in which Pat attempts to reassert various commonly shared rules for the household.) Not fully awake, the teenagers are, at best, unenthusiastic about school, disparaging their homework assignments. In episode ten, after his first day back at school in September, Grant tells his mother that he "hated every minute of it."

The breakfast scene shows the family living together before Bill and

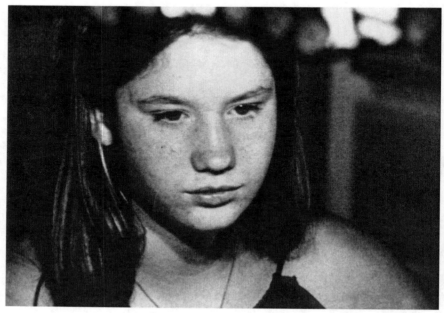

Michele Loud in episode one of *An American Family.*

Pat separated. A different shot showcases each family member's "entrance" to the dining room, allowing the viewer to identify each clearly. (Whenever possible, characters exit the frame before the program cuts to another shot, smoothing transitions.) All of the action in this scene takes place in the kitchen and the dining room. Although some of the images are taken from the same camera angle, the framing varies enough to allow the scene to flow smoothly. There are thirty-four shots; the average lasts approximately thirteen seconds, relatively short for an observational documentary. The handheld camera remains steady throughout. Sounds flow across image cuts to create and maintain continuous spatial and temporal relations.

When Bill addresses his youngest child—"Do you hear those birds singing out there these days, Michele?"—he looks screen right, in the direction of the kitchen. In the following shot, Michele, in the kitchen, looks screen left, acknowledging his words. The sounds and images reinforce one another; after we hear Bill and Pat refer to Michele's health, a shot shows their daughter gently touching her throat. The editing maintains continuity through eye-line matches, overlapping sound cuts, point-of-view shots, and cutting on action. (There are jump cuts, however, such as the consecutive shots of Grant, and the transitions in general are not as smooth as in fiction films. Furthermore, the production values, especially the lighting and handheld camera, remain those of verité documentary.) The cutting strategy condenses time and space, without calling attention to the ellipses, through a panoply of continuity techniques. An event that lasts up to an hour in real time takes only seven and a half minutes of screen time, yet nothing significant has been left out. The family sets the table, cooks breakfast, eats, cleans up, and leaves. As Pat casually glances out the kitchen window, a point-of-view shot from her perspective shows the children leaving for school. (Like the other devices, the POV shot helps create a coherent filmic space.) Their departure in a pickup truck ends the sequence, and the episode cuts to an establishing shot of the Chelsea Hotel in New York. A new scene begins.

With several exceptions already mentioned, *An American Family* constructs scenes, stories, and episodes through narrative techniques common to fictional film and television. Viewers discover the plot, and the point of view of the program, through the actions and words of the characters and the juxtaposition of scenes. Although observational sequences seemingly represent life on the run, the series exhibits a fascinating, and subtle, narrative sophistication. The teleological structure sets up the longest flashback—eleven and a half hours—in the history of motion pictures and strongly asserts a narrative chain of causes and effects. The multiple-focus narrative intersperses story developments among many characters, allowing for suspense, delay, and anticipation. Within this structure, transitions between otherwise unrelated scenes remain key moments for expressing editorial perspective. In the next chapter, through a closer consideration of the role of sound in *An American Family,* I will demonstrate the similarities and differences of observational cinema in respect to both Hollywood films and traditional documentaries.

[5] Sound in Documentary: Listening to the Louds

Most analyses of films and TV programs accent their visual dimensions to the detriment of sound. True for both fiction and nonfiction, such emphasis seriously underestimates the role of sound on television. Whereas traditional documentaries use sound for purposes of direct address, observational cinema offers a subtler use of sound textures, more comparable to fiction film. However, although observational tracks include words, music, and ambient sounds, the hierarchy and distribution of these sounds differ in important ways from their use in Hollywood features. In fact, the studio division of sound into discrete dialogue, music, and effects tracks obscures the extent to which these are integral parts of documentary sound. Film theorist Rick Altman has described the conventions of sound in classical Hollywood cinema as an interplay between intelligibility and fidelity to the real world, a system in which fidelity is sacrificed in favor of the more narratively central dimension of intelligibility.[1]

Similarly, philosopher Noël Carroll argues that the hallmark of Hollywood movie narration is clarity and comprehensibility. Popular movies offer experiences of places, events, characters, and drama more clearly delineated than our ordinary lives. In Carroll's words: "The flow of action approaches an ideal of uncluttered clarity. This clarity contrasts vividly with the quality of fragments of actions and events we typically observe in everyday life."[2] Hollywood filmmakers use techniques of image and sound to focus the attention of the spectator on the salient elements that further the narrative. Carroll suggests that it is not the purported realism of the cinematic apparatus that millions of viewers find compelling, but rather the heightened intelligibility that represents the hallmark of Hollywood cinema. If audiences were truly interested in greater fidelity to the world, then presumably documentary films would form a larger part of the corpus that made motion pictures a very popular art form in the twentieth century.

Documentaries rarely demonstrate the degree of clarity that Altman and Carroll see as the standard of classical Hollywood cinema. Location sound work in nonfiction occasionally makes discrimination among sounds difficult, if not impossible. The intelligibility of observational cinema rarely approaches that of popular movies; characters lack clear motivations, speech may be inaudible in parts, lighting can be haphazard and variable, camera movements follow actions with difficulty, sound spaces differ radically between scenes, microphones accidentally appear in the image, jump cuts disrupt continuity, and questions remain unanswered. In this chapter, I present a survey of the role of sound in documentary, and in *An American Family* in particular, before considering ways in which Gilbert's series takes liberties with the observational style. I conclude by detailing reflexive moments when the Louds, or the program itself, acknowledge the presence of an audience.

▶

Location Sound

Observational cinema transformed documentary narration primarily through new location sound recording techniques, approaches that added realism while simultaneously demanding greater attention from viewers. A low signal-to-noise ratio, for example, makes it more difficult to decipher words spoken in situ. Slight differences in room tone between shots make smooth sound transitions difficult. Ambient sounds compete with dialogue in ways commonly deemed unacceptable in conventional Hollywood practice. Indeed, listening to many of the scenes of *An American Family* without watching the screen can be a dizzying experience. Without recognizable sources in the image to anchor the sounds, a virtual cacophony arises, snippets of dialogue, music, and various unidentifiable noises, almost an experiment in concrete music. Because sequences in observational films are not shot under optimal conditions, such as those found in a Hollywood studio, the sound lacks directness.

Film production in the United States moved inside studios around 1908 to avoid the kinds of uncertainties encountered in actuality and location filmmaking.[3] Today, mass-production techniques and a precise division of labor ensure the technical quality of Hollywood sound. Repeated takes are done until satisfactory sound has been recorded; if necessary, dialogue is postproduced through dubbing to ensure clarity. Fiction directors shoot individual shots one at a time under optimal conditions in studios, whereas documentary filmmakers often record entire sequences in long takes under unpredictable circumstances. Similarly, Hollywood composers write musical scores to match perfectly the action on the screen. In fiction films, the degree of direct, as opposed to reflected, sound indicates the level of control exercised over all aspects of recording. The brilliance of sound practice in the classical Hollywood cinema derives from a combination of direct sound, closely miked in order to reduce reverberation and increase clarity, with an overall system of impersonal narration.[4]

The clarity of sound in documentary often depends on the degree of command the filmmaker has over the situation. Spoken narration allows for maximum control over quality, and voice-over has long been one of the stylistic signatures of nonfiction sound. Post-verité documentaries—such as *Sherman's March* (1986), Ross McElwee's parody civil war documentary, and *Roger & Me* (1989), Michael Moore's first-person critique of General Motors—have rediscovered the possibilities of voice-over narration, using personal, ironic, and interpretive commentary to counterpoint location-recorded images and sounds. In these films, spoken narration is more than just a necessary concession to the needs of exposition and storytelling. In Hollywood cinema, voice-over has long been considered "the last resort of the incompetent," a view shared by many observational documentary filmmakers.[5] When Leacock and Pincus taught nonfiction filmmaking at MIT in the 1970s, voice-over was not considered an acceptable technique. Spoken narration in fiction films often serves as a marker of documentary authenticity, as in John Ford's *How Green Was My Valley* (1941), Anthony Mann's *T-Men* (1947), and Jules Dassin's *The Naked City* (1948).

▶──

Speech

Characters in nonfiction films typically demonstrate a wider variety of accents, dialects, and speech patterns than those found in fiction films. In their discussion of the documentaries of Frederick Wiseman, communication scholars Thomas Benson and Carolyn Anderson see this breadth as a marker of truth to reality: "No other filmmaker has more to say to us about the American language than Frederick Wiseman. In film after film he has shown us the structure and uses of the American idiom, inviting us to listen, at length, to conversational passages that most other filmmakers would have left on the cutting-room floor."[6] Although this breadth promotes a rich diversity, it presents obstacles for the viewer's understanding. Regional accents, slang, and idiosyncratic syntax make nonfictional representations of speech more difficult to grasp than their fictional counterparts. Pincus chose to subtitle the conversations of some of the children who appear in *Black Natchez* (1967), his film about civil rights struggles in Mississippi.

(Such subtitling, however, often implies deviance from a linguistic norm.) Observational documentaries often do not succeed outside their national boundaries because of the difficulties presented for viewers who are not native speakers of the language. Part of the delight of watching documentaries comes from hearing the material texture and richness of unrehearsed speech, the grain of the voice.

Speakers in everyday life typically fill in the gaps of their phrases with various exclamations and sounds that maintain the flow of verbal communication. In conversation, we interrupt one another, digress, ask questions, hem and haw. Telephone conversations exemplify these characteristics. The absence of nonverbal cues necessitates a constant use of verbal signals to indicate that the listener is in fact awake and listening. Much verbal communication consists of what sociolinguist Dell Hymes calls the phatic function of speech, the banal pitter-patter that signifies sociability, "talk for the sake of something being said."[7] Anyone who has ever transcribed interview tapes recognizes the differences between spoken and written language. Characters in Hollywood films speak scripted versions of spoken language and are careful not to interrupt one another's lines. In addition, from one take to another, actors must maintain identical volume, pitch, tone, and inflection for continuity purposes, a talent for which they are handsomely paid. Dialogue in observational documentaries overlaps considerably, as characters interrupt one another, speak at the same time, and affirm their listening stances. As film historian Michel Marie remarks of synchronous sound techniques, "Direct [cinema] is really a manifestation of a new modality of voice recording in film."[8]

Interview films attempt to circumvent the fullness of ordinary speech in various ways. Staged to be recorded, interviews may be miked for maximum intelligibility. Documentary makers learn how to set up interviews so that interviewees will appear to speak directly to the viewer. Producer Michael Rabiger instructs would-be filmmakers in his textbook *Directing the Documentary:* "During the interview, you should maintain eye contact with your subject, and give visual (NOT verbal!) feedback while the interview goes on. Nodding, smiling, looking puzzled, signifying agreement or doubt are all forms of feedback that can be relayed through your expression."[9] In the *New Yorker*, Errol Morris, director of *The Thin Blue Line* (1988), described the importance of providing these nonverbal cues: "Listening to what people were saying wasn't even important. But it was important to *look* as if you were listening to what people were saying. Actually, listening to what people are saying, to me, interferes with looking as if you were listening to what people were saying."[10] Interview films increase the clarity and directness of speech through editing techniques and shooting conventions.

British TV scholar Roger Silverstone makes note of this process in the shooting of a BBC documentary, in which the director instructs the interviewee to answer in full sentences so that the questions may be left out of the sound track.

> M: Say that again because you spoke while I was speaking.
> L: Stability is the key word in terms of what he is . . . .
> M: So he's a tougher judge than scientific colleagues almost?
> L: Exactly.
> M: Say that again from the start.
> L: What, about the . . . ?
> M: Yes, as a sentence.[11]

Interview films permit a mise-en-scène of speech, a trimming of the materiality of conversational speech in favor of clarity and comprehensibility.

In the 1970s and 1980s, independent documentary filmmakers returned to the direct-address style of interview films in part because it allowed them greater control over what was happening in front of the camera. Political documentaries such as *The Good Fight* (Noel Buckner, Mary Dore, and Sam Sills, 1983), an oral history of American volunteers who fought for the Republican cause in Spain, used techniques that allow for more thorough preparation during preproduction. The use of a string of interviews permits a strong sense of textual voice, not unlike that of a voice-over, dispersed across multiple characters.[12] Although voice-over narration and interviews allow for more direct sound in documentary, they remain marginal techniques in observational cinema. "Interviews" that appear in observational works are carried out by characters who appear in the films, such as the psychiatrists in Wiseman's *Titicut Follies* (1967) who interrogate incoming patients about their medical histories, thereby introducing viewers to both the characters and the procedures of the institution.

Location sound recording in observational documentary does not clearly differentiate foreground and background spaces; rather, all sounds compete together in the middle ground. While perhaps aiding claims of realism, the lack of clarity compromises these works. Occasionally in observational films, poorly recorded scenes appear because of their central importance to the story. In *An American Family,* a conversation between Bill and Pat at a crowded restaurant is virtually inaudible due to the presence of competing ambient sounds. A determined viewer may overcome the marginal sound quality to catch snippets of their argument, an important indication of the downturn of their marriage. Pat's comments are the harshest heard throughout the series: "I think that the things that you do are shitty. And perhaps you think that the things I do are shitty, that's your problem. But I think that you're a goddamn asshole." Although the sound is muddled, the point is clear.

▶

Music

Music plays an important part in nonfiction films and television programs. Network producer David Wolper acknowledged its indispensable role in his work: "CBS said for a while, 'No music in documentaries.' I looked at them like they were crazy. I said, 'What do you mean, "no music"? Let's have no words, I mean, music is just another form—another adjective on the page.' Music, you know, creates the emotion."[13] Famous composers, such as Benjamin Britten and Virgil Thomson, scored many of the classic documentaries of the 1930s, including Harry Watt's *Night Mail* (1936) and Pare Lorentz's *The River* (1937). Highlighting the importance of sound in their titles, Dziga Vertov's *Three Songs of Lenin* (1934), Basil Wright's *Song of Ceylon* (1934), and Humphrey Jennings's *Listen to Britain* (1942) make extensive use of music. The on-camera host who introduces *Listen to Britain,* on the 16mm print in distribution in North America, calls attention to "the first sure notes of the march of victory, as you and I listen to Britain."

Film historian Stephen Mamber suggests that observational filmmakers in the 1960s moved away from these techniques: "In line with this commitment, some of the standard devices of fiction film and traditional documentaries fall by the wayside, especially music and [voice-over] narration."[14] Although the rhetoric of observational cinema demanded the use of images and sounds recorded during shooting, the new approach did not preclude the use of music. On the contrary, music was fine as long as it was recorded on location, and throughout the 1960s there was plenty of music in observational films. In fact, the documentary musical emerged as a distinct subgenre, focusing primarily on the sounds of rock and roll.

Just as the coming of sound fostered the growth of the Hollywood musical in the 1930s, innovations in location sound recording technology led to the rock documentary in the 1960s. The Maysleses' *What's Happening! The Beatles in the U.S.A.* (1964) and *Gimme Shelter* (1970; the Rolling Stones in concert at Altamont in 1969), Pennebaker's *Don't Look Back* (1967; Bob Dylan on tour in England in 1965) and *Monterey Pop* (1969; performances by Janis Joplin, Jimi Hendrix, and others at the 1967 Monterey Pop Festival), and Michael Wadleigh's *Woodstock* (1970) put

A publicity still from Michael Wadleigh's *Woodstock.*

musicians center stage. The rock documentary brings together nonfiction film's traditional focus on actuality and the fictional cinema's emphasis on stars and spectacle. Even Wiseman's *Titicut Follies,* a study of a mental institution, uses a musical revue performed by the patients as a framing device, a carnivalesque inversion and parody of the music documentary, in which the patients sing "Have You Ever Been Lonely?," "I Want to Go to Chicagotown," and "So Long For Now." Still today, music documentaries are among the most commercially successful of nonfiction forms, with popular works such as Jonathan Demme's concert film about the Talking Heads, *Stop Making Sense* (1984), and Alek Keshishian's portrait of Madonna, *Truth or Dare* (1991). The canonization of the form came with Rob Reiner's parody of a British heavy metal band on tour, *This Is Spinal Tap* (1984).

Recorded music appears frequently in observational documentaries. As in the early days of sound film, a shot of a radio or record player often signals its on-screen source. Although filmmakers want to indicate that musical segments were found on location for aesthetic reasons, this practice also results from legal and financial concerns. Some believe that they should not be obliged to pay users' fees to music copyright owners. At the 1990 Ohio Film Conference, Wiseman argued that his extensive use of location-recorded music by bands like the B-52s in *Model* (1980), for which no fees were paid, would be defensible in court. Negotiating for the rights to use music is a notoriously difficult and expensive process, forcing some filmmakers to avoid such sequences altogether.[15]

In *An American Family*, Pat languishes by her swimming pool the day after she asked her husband to move out of the house. In an adjoining bedroom, in a crosscut scene, Delilah listens to the strains of Carole King's "Will You Love Me Tomorrow?" As the music carries over to images of Pat curled up in a lounge chair, the bitterness of the separation is amplified. The program cuts back and forth between Delilah, making herself up in front of a bathroom mirror, and her mother at the pool as King sings of enduring treasures versus momentary pleasures, lines that apply not only to Pat, but also to her maturing fifteen-year-old daughter. This scene neatly echoes that of Bill and his new lover dancing on New Year's Eve in episode one as a piano man croons King's "You've Got a Friend," which also appears on King's *Tapestry* album. (In episode seven, during an argument with Bill, Pat quotes a tune then very much on the airwaves: "Too late now. You know that song? That Carole King song: 'Too Late Baby.'") Although documentary filmmakers imply in interviews that such incidents simply happen and are just happy coincidences, their use clearly demonstrates an authorial intention on the part of the makers, a sense of aesthetic and thematic unity, and an implicit point of view. The music provides an editorial perspective

Pat Loud in episode nine of *An American Family.*

for interpreting the images, which is the function of narrative film music in general.[16]

Although the conventions of observational film require that music be recorded on location, the role of music in the narrative structure of these films appears quite similar to the role of music in classical Hollywood cinema. Music provides continuity, covers up edits, facilitates changes of scenes, helps establish time and place, provides mood, offers entertaining spectacle, allows for narrative interludes or montage sequences, and comments on the action. (Eleven episodes of *An American Family* open with the theme song, and ten end with music over the credits.) Wiseman begins *High School* (1969) with a car radio playing Otis Redding's "Dock of the Bay" and the chorus about "wasting time" comes to stand for the experience of students at Northeast High.[17] By and large, nonfiction filmmakers work as rigorously as their Hollywood counterparts to find musical passages that contribute to the narrative and thematic concerns of their films. Barbara Kopple's *Harlan County, U.S.A.* (1976) profits from a rich and moving sample of folk songs that shows music to be a repository of community and memory in the Kentucky miners' struggle for their civil rights.

The new conventions of observational documentary in the 1960s required that filmmakers discover musical selections in the original scenes they recorded. Not surprisingly, the ordinary people who populate observational documentaries often play music themselves. In Marc Obenhaus's "The Pasciaks of Chicago" (1976) episode from the television series *Six American Families,* the son's dedication to rock music creates tensions within his Polish working-class family; his mother wants him to play polkas on the accordion, and his interest in rock and roll reflects his attempt to assimilate into mainstream pop culture. Similarly, the new cadets in Joan Churchill and Nick Broomfield's *Soldier Girls* (1981) perform a lively rap tune in the barracks during a break in their basic training sessions in Georgia.

In *An American Family,* young Grant Loud diligently plucks away on his guitar and sings in a budding garage band with his brother Kevin. During the twelve-hour series, the band performs the Rolling Stones' "Jumpin' Jack Flash" and "Brown Sugar" and Eddie Cochran's "Summertime Blues," made famous by The Who. These regular appearances culminate in an amusing parody of rock concerts—"a kind of satire on rock and roll," in Grant's words—staged by the band at a pep rally at Santa Barbara High School in episode ten. With his friends cheering in mock hysteria, Grant arrives on a motorcycle, wearing black tights, a skin-tight black shirt, and a cape, to sing of teenage love in Bonzo Dog Doo-Dah Band's "Tent."

This sequence shows how thoroughly Grant, Kevin, and their friends had absorbed the ecstatic performance style of Mick Jagger, which is canonized in *Gimme Shelter*. At the same time, it demonstrates a critical distance on the part of Grant and his cohorts from the conventions of pop music. (It also suggests that the value of music as entertainment and spectacle was recognized by the producers of *An American Family*.) Later, Grant serenades his mother in the living room with an acoustic version of the Kinks' "Ape Man," announcing, "It's entertainment time at the Loud house. Will you get situated, please." As with "Won't Get Fooled Again" and John Lennon's "Imagine," also heard on the sound track, the lyrics provide overt sociopolitical commentary, in this case a tongue-in-cheek utopian return to primitive life. Delilah then requests that her brother play the Beatles' "Mother Nature's Son," another song that romanticizes the noble savage.[18]

▶

Breaking the Rules

Although *An American Family* may be the most famous example of observational cinema, it deviates, usually through sound techniques, from the proscriptive rules of that style. Gilbert occasionally flaunts his omniscience in the voice-over, anticipating future story events, as in episode eight: "It is September 2nd, the day before Bill is due back in Santa Barbara. Pat has

Mick Jagger in a publicity still for the Maysleses' *Gimme Shelter*.

decided to file for divorce, and has told her children. Later in the day she will drive to Glendale to explain her feelings to her brother, Tom, and his wife Yvonne." The tracking shot of Pat that accompanies this passage ends as she enters a door marked "Frank R. Crandall, Attorney at Law."

Coordinating producer Jacqueline Donnet described the decision to use this voice-over as a trade-off between the comprehensibility of the narrative and the conventions of observational film:

> There is a scene in the show where she tells her brother that she is going to divorce Bill, that she wants to separate and get a divorce. That was the other time that we wrenched the convention of not telling you, by telling you up front that she was driving down to speak to her brother about the divorce. The main reason for that was the sound track is so garbled. It's very hard to hear. Our feeling was that you miss half of it and all of a sudden realize what she is saying and you haven't heard the front half. So that was the other time we pinpointed something.

In addition to Gilbert's voice-over, both Mr. and Mrs. Loud narrate first-person voice-over passages. In episode four, Pat speaks her words haltingly, as if reading from a script or answering off-screen questions. Her voice lacks any specific room tone, and the sound is uncharacteristically clear. She is literally not speaking in her own voice; a photograph taken during postproduction shows Pat Loud and Craig Gilbert composing the narration for this sequence, a stopwatch and film projector within view. The rehearsed style of her speech contrasts vividly with the spontaneity of her voice in the observational scenes of her daily life; her inexperience as a narrator becomes a touching sign of the authenticity of her routine appearances in front of the camera.

Similarly, in episode eleven, Bill reads in voice-over a letter that he wrote to Lance shortly after his separation from Pat. No ambient sound accompanies his words as images show his eldest son bicycling through Santa Barbara. "Dearest Lance, thank you for your wonderful letter, I thoroughly enjoyed it. The contents were well constructed and I very much enjoyed your analogy of the return of Lance versus the fall of the father." This device allows Bill to express his feelings about the split directly: "I really have no desire to return home. Loneliness is not one of my problems and I want to see if I can forge a new life for myself that I have considered for some time." His delivery shares the same awkward qualities as Pat's voice-over.

Prerecorded music also occasionally surfaces in Gilbert's series. When Lance travels to Paris, an accordion plays in the background. The clarity of the music suggests it was not taped on location. Needless to say, accordion music provides the most conventional associations with France. *An American Family* also offers canned music with the silent home-movie scenes Pat

Craig Gilbert and Pat Loud work on *An American Family*. Used by permission of *Studies in Visual Communication*.

describes in voice-over. A toy musical box accompanies these images of childhood lost; "Jingle Bells" plays on a child's organ during footage of Christmas celebrations. Evocative sounds of cooing babies fade in and out, the echoes of bygone days. Another sequence of home movies, shot in Brazil, where Pat lived as a young girl, unfolds with generic samba music in the background.

The home movies and family photographs themselves represent an important detour from the observational focus on images and sounds recorded in the present. The Louds' home movies chronicle festive occasions such as Thanksgiving dinners and baby Lance taking his first steps. These nostalgic recollections suggest happier times, offering a powerful contrast to the Louds' contemporary lives. The *New York Times Magazine* reviewer, novelist Anne Roiphe, perceptively noted the result: "As the photographs and home movies showed on the screen with occasional explanatory comment from Pat or her mother, I was shaken with a particularly searing kind of sadness."[19] Roiphe, however, failed to identify the formal cues involved: home movies and observational cinema are antithetical documentary modes. Home movies from the summer of 1971 could have been equally touching in comparison to the Raymonds' footage. One common criticism of observational cinema is that it fails to deal adequately with the past, a limitation that Gilbert overcomes here through other means of expression—interviews, voice-over narration, canned music, photographs, and home movies.

▶

Reflexivity and Observational Cinema

Like fiction films, observational documentaries employ an impersonal narration that does not explicitly address the viewer. Nevertheless, anyone who actually watches *An American Family,* even just a single episode, witnesses numerous references to the audience. These moments call our attention to the fact that we are watching a film, reminding us that it was produced by a crew. Too many to catalog, these are not the first elements viewers notice, or the last. Thus Gilbert's style falls between the overt reflexivity of French cinema verité director Jean Rouch and the transparent observational style of Frederick Wiseman.

In episode four, an amusing discussion takes place about the proper way to display mayonnaise on the table at 35 Wooddale Lane, calling attention to differences between public and private behavior. Pat invokes proper standards for entertaining guests, "You're supposed to put it in a dish and not put the jar on the table." Her good-humored children refuse to participate in this charade and ignore her remonstrations, implicitly welcoming the filmmakers as members of the household. Alone in Bill's office in episode eleven, Lance finds a letter he wrote to his father and reads it aloud to the camera: "There are two things you can count on in life, as the world turns. They are that at the end of the summer Lance always returns from an unsuccessful takeoff on life's big runway, limping home on a path of wired money. And Ma and Pa Loud plummet headfirst from their Olympian heights of love and matrimony." Lance acknowledges the melodramatic associations of the documentary through his comparison of his family's experiences to *As the World Turns* (1956–present). Only Mr. Loud's sudden return to his workplace interrupts this remarkable frame-breaking soliloquy.

In episode eight, Bill confesses his worries about Lance traveling in Europe to his colleagues in strip-mining, but his fears are dispelled by the fact that, as he remarks, "They have the camera crew with them over there, following them around!" After an argument with Michele in the driveway in hour six, Pat smiles at the camera and says, "Lost another skirmish." In episode three, as Delilah and her boyfriend flirt in the background, Grant passes in front of the camera and says, in a theatrical whisper, "Brad and Delilah Love Scene, Part Two." In hour eleven, Bill and Lance pose together, arm in arm, as Kevin prepares to take a photograph. Shooting from over Kevin's shoulder, the cinematographer frames them in like manner and Bill's question, "Are we in focus, Kevin?" might just as easily apply to the 16mm movie camera in Alan Raymond's hands. In addition, as Kevin snaps the picture, the action freezes like a photograph and the credits roll.

Additional reflexive gestures include references to other films and television shows. Several scenes feature one or more of the Louds watching TV. In each case, the dialogue on the television set contributes to the marital focus of *An American Family*. In hour nine—in which Pat tells Bill that she wants a divorce—Michele watches an old black-and-white Hollywood western. A woman perched on a horse says, "What do you know about women?" Her male companion replies, "I guess nobody knows about women, but I know a lot about men." In episode eleven, looking for an evening's entertainment in the newspaper, Grant suggests *Carnal Knowledge* (Mike Nichols, 1971) or *The Hellstrom Chronicle* (Walon Green and Ed Spiegel, 1971). He adds that the latter, which won an Academy Award for Best Documentary that year, has "not a very original plot."

These ubiquitous references to the filmmaking process go beyond those of other observational works from the same period, predating similar instances in, for example, Albert and David Maysles's *Grey Gardens* (1975). Film theorists who denounce observational documentaries as transparent forms that disguise the work of mediation, such as E. Ann Kaplan, would do well to look closely at *An American Family*.[20] If a fictional series from 1973 had used these devices, such critics would have hailed it as a major breakthrough in Brechtian television.

The single most reflexive element of *An American Family* is Lance Loud, who relentlessly breaks frame, acknowledging the presence of the camera throughout the twelve-hour series. Reviewers, writing in newspapers and magazines, did not know what to do with Lance and his send-up of documentary conventions. Unlike the more naturalistic performances of his siblings and parents, Lance acts like a character from an Andy Warhol movie loose in a film by Frederick Wiseman. A fan of Warhol's work, Lance turns in one of the great camp performances in the history of television. In *Heavenly Bodies*, Richard Dyer defines camp as a "characteristically gay way of handling the values, images and products of the dominant culture through irony, exaggeration, trivialization, theatricalization, and an ambivalent making fun of and out of the serious and respectable."[21] Shooting Super-8 footage on a Santa Barbara beach in episode twelve, Lance tells his cast of friends, "Realism is our aim for this film; it's going to be like a documentary." But his directions verge on camp horror: "Okay, now a close-up of you looking like a hungry sex-devil." Probably the first openly gay character ever featured on American TV, Lance consistently makes fun

Lance and Michele Loud in *An American Family.*

of the serious pretensions of the documentary, undermining the codes of observational cinema. These reflexive moments encourage audience members to think about *An American Family* as a representation and, in the process, to recognize that in any documentary there is "an interaction between filmer and subject."[22]

III   The Reception of
An American Family

[**6**] Publicity Sets the Stage, Reviews Steal the Show

Viewers built their weeks around An American Family
because it was like watching live soap opera.
:: Alice Carey, production secretary

For three months during the winter of 1973, beginning on January 11, American audiences settled down to watch the lives of the Louds in sunny Santa Barbara. *An American Family* was one of the most popular documentaries ever broadcast. Although it is impossible to reconstruct the varied reactions of millions of viewers (who left no written traces of their responses), the series offers an excellent case study of how reviewers understand and interpret nonfiction. Under normal circumstances, many television critics do little other than regurgitate the information contained in production company press packets. Gilbert's series, however, was far from a normal TV program, making the publicity campaign both more important than usual (reviewers desperately needed critical terms to rely on) and less important than usual (in the absence of a shared vocabulary, a semiological free-for-all resulted). Viewing patterns, coupled with attitudes about television, also played a crucial role in the way the program was watched, interpreted, and criticized. In the early 1970s, TV did not have a reputation as a serious art form, a reputation movies had only recently acquired.

Although nonfiction filmmakers often aspire to have real-world impacts on viewers, surprisingly few scholars of documentary have written about issues of reception. Debates about the purpose and nature of nonfiction usually center on analyses of individual films and the merits of specific stylistic devices, such as voice-over narration. In other words, like most of film studies, such discussions are based on the films themselves. Visual anthropologist Jay Ruby claims that documentaries mask their ideological agendas, fooling viewers into thinking they are watching objective representations of the world. Using this, albeit untested, theory of spectatorship, Ruby has argued in a series of articles for a self-reflexive documentary that would acknowledge its constructed nature.[1] If Ruby is right, viewers of documentaries fail to grasp the mediation involved in nonfiction; they appreciate the films as essentially transparent renditions of the world.

More recently, film theorist Bill Nichols, while surely sympathetic to Ruby's formulation, has offered another text-based definition of nonfiction film. In *Representing Reality,* Nichols maintains that documentaries may best be categorized as works that present an "argument about the historical world."[2] Although Nichols's claim may hold true for didactic shows such as CBS's *Harvest of Shame* (David Lowe, 1960), it remains to be seen whether this description fits observational cinema. If Nichols is right, viewers understand documentaries to be persuasive constructions with explicit points of view. The disparate reactions to Gilbert's series offer contradictory evidence: Ruby's notion of the naive viewer accurately describes most of the published responses to the program, while a vocal minority clearly read the series as an argument about contemporary life. Furthermore, the tremendous preoccupation with the making of *An American Family* suggests an implicit understanding that the program was a construction, not a transparent window.

▶

WNET's Publicity Campaign

TV and film critics do not write reviews in a vacuum. The WNET press packet laid out terms reviewers could borrow to characterize the Louds without even watching the show. WNET circulated a review essay by Fredelle Maynard with the press packet: "The breakdown in communications in the Loud family is perhaps a typical American disease, the result of disproportionate emphasis on maintaining surfaces, keeping cool. These people meet without touching, touch without meeting."[3] Although not produced by Gilbert or his principal collaborators, the press portfolio defined the purview of the series. It set the stage, and most of the terms, for published responses to the program, especially given that it was more didactic than the documentary itself. The publicity campaign established a horizon of expectations—a set of thematic and generic categories—for television critics and viewers. Many early reviews amounted to little more than publicity, confirming Alan Raymond's comment that "most television critics just take a press release and run with it." This symbiotic relationship plagues reception studies, such as Janet Staiger's *Interpreting Films,* that fail to consider the reciprocal relationship between advertising and reviewing.[4]

The publicity campaign created the first impressions of the series,

This is Lance Loud, public television's flamboyant 21-year-old member of "An American Family." The 12-week cinema verite examination of a Santa Barbara, California family airs weekly over the Public Broadcasting Service on Thursdays at 9:00 p.m. (Please check your local PBS station for area broadcast time.) Lance now lives in New York City's Greenwich Village.

Lance Loud in a WNET publicity photograph.

which were then reinforced by reviewers. Given the intermittent and distracted nature of television viewing, this first impression greatly influenced responses to *An American Family*. The WNET press packet contrasted the documentary with the depiction of families on situation comedies and soap operas, thus supplying crucial references.[5] The idea that the program scrutinized the American dream appeared first in the WNET portfolio: "The members of the Loud family have been shaped by the national myths and promises, the American dream and experiences that affect all of us, whether we be rich or poor, black or white, young or old."[6] The press release argued for a commonsense notion of shared American identity that was, at the time, very much under attack from revisionist historians and social activists.[7]

For the benefit of reviewers, the press materials established the family as rich and materialistic, linked not by bonds of love but by modern communications systems. The "Profile of the William C. Loud Family" accentuated their family's social status to the point of caricature:

The Louds live in a modern eight-room stucco ranch house. Set on a scenic mountain drive amid the lush shrubbery and trees of southern California, the

Loud home serves as the headquarters for the well-traveled family. (Pat may be in Eugene, Ore., while Lance is in Paris and Kevin is in Australia, but all seven Louds remain very much in touch with each other through regular phone calls to the Santa Barbara "message center.")

When the family is home, they are often joined by friends for gracious dinner parties, rock-group rehearsals, class meetings or a swim in the pool. When they leave their house, the Louds are able to choose a means of transportation from among the four vehicles they own: a Jaguar, Volvo, Toyota and Datsun pickup truck. In addition to its seven human inhabitants, the Loud household is alive with a pack of family pets including a horse, three dogs (a large crossbreed and two standard poodles), two cats and a bowl of goldfish.[8]

The use of the words "headquarters" and "message center" suggested that the house was a soulless corporation rather than a home, and the emphasis on travel hinted at a mobile, rootless, nuclear family, unattached to other social institutions. The sheer number of cars highlighted the family's affluence, as did mention of the pool and horse. The press portfolio associated the American dream, through the medium of the Louds, to the pursuit of wealth and the consumption of material goods.

The publicity campaign consistently referred to the subjects as the "William C. Loud family," a practice followed by reviewers. *An American*

Mr. and Mrs. William C. Loud of Santa Barbara, California. Bill, 50, his wife Pat, 45, and their five children are the subjects of AN AMERICAN FAMILY, WNET/13's landmark series of 12 hour-long documentaries. Producer Craig Gilbert and his camera crews spent seven months living with the Louds, recording their day-to-day lives. AN AMERICAN FAMILY, a unique panorama of contemporary American life, premieres in New York on WNET/13 and nationally over the Public Broadcasting Service on Thursday, January 11 at 9:00 p.m. (Please check your local PBS station for area broadcast time.)

"Mr. and Mrs. William C. Loud" in a WNET publicity photograph.

Family did not sustain this image of patriarchal control, given that it placed much more emphasis on Pat and Lance than on Bill. Referring to the family in this way served a conscious ironic function, as the series chronicled the demise of the "William C. Loud family." The WNET press packet included a portrait of the Louds, with all the family members dressed up for the occasion, together with two of their dogs, smiling at the camera. The Louds had made this photograph for their 1971 Christmas card and, as such, it represented the antithesis of the spontaneous observational style. The photo offered a view of happy middle-class family life that *An American Family* deliberately challenged; its circulation in the press packet set up another ironic contrast for reviewers. The photograph was widely reprinted in the publicity campaign for the documentary, appearing weekly with advertisements in the *New York Times.*

Although the producer avoided using an on-camera host, interviews, and voice-over narration, the press release nevertheless provided an explanatory framework for *An American Family:* "Gilbert has attempted to answer some of the larger questions about modern American society: What

The Loud family in a WNET publicity photograph.

A portrait of the William C. Loud family of Santa Barbara, California, subjects of AN AMERICAN FAMILY, WNET/13's landmark series of 12 hour-long documentaries. From the left: (front row) Michele, 13; Pat, 45; and Bill, 50; (back row) Kevin, 18; Grant, 17; Delilah, 15; and Lance, 20. Producer Craig Gilbert and his camera crews spent seven months living with the Loud family and recording their day-to-day lives. AN AMERICAN FAMILY, a unique panorama of contemporary life, premieres in New York on WNET/13 and nationally over the Public Broadcasting Service on Thursday, January 11 at 9:00 p.m. (Please check your local PBS station for area broadcast time).

is the current American Dream? Why has marriage become something less than a permanent arrangement? What is left of the parent-child relationship? Where are America's children going?"[9] The publicity materials contradicted Gilbert's desire to show family life without telling viewers what to think, to present what the associate producer called "the discomfort of the real." The observational style implied that viewers could decide for themselves about the Louds; the press packet, however, made clear that the family, and by implication the country, was in trouble.

The advertising campaign that ran in newspapers across the country served a similar function. The first ad appeared in the January 11 edition of the *New York Times* for the evening broadcast of episode one. Bold capital letters asked, "ARE YOU READY FOR 'AN AMERICAN FAMILY'?" underneath the same Christmas photograph, suggesting that something outrageous was coming on PBS. By this time, the Louds' divorce was no secret. The January 6 issue of *TV Guide* simply noted, "Eight months after the filming was completed, the marriage had ended in divorce."[10] Of course, the press packet provided this information, "During the filming of *An American Family,* the Louds' 20-year marriage collapsed, ending in a separation."[11] Viewers, then, were liable to know the general outline of the program before ever tuning in to the broadcast.

The advertisement in the *New York Times* for the second episode on January 18 was even more inflammatory. Bold capital letters proclaimed, "HE DYED HIS HAIR SILVER" for the episode that focused on Lance Loud. Lance's face appeared torn out of the Christmas photograph, segregating him from the rest of the family. "He lives in the Chelsea Hotel on Manhattan's lower West Side. And lives a lifestyle that might shock a lot of people back home in California." The advertisement exploited Lance's sexual orientation, hinting that he dyed his clothes purple "as a personal expression of . . . something . . . something he wasn't fully aware of at the time." Probably influenced by this ad campaign, many critics claimed, erroneously, that Lance "came out" on TV.

Through the ideological work of the press materials, Lance became the repressed nightmare of what John J. O'Connor called the Louds' image of "toothpaste-bright affluence."[12] As journalist Merle Miller acknowledged in *Esquire,* in a response that says much about the way the series and Lance's place in it were constructed, Lance was "hardly what we've been brought up to think is the All-American boy."[13] In the *New York Times Magazine,* novelist Anne Roiphe expressed surprise that the Louds showed no "open horror" at Lance's sexual orientation.[14] Responding to Roiphe and others, Miller—author of *On Being Different: What It Means to Be a Homosexual,* a work one can easily imagine Pat or Lance reading at the time—wrote positively about the family, arguing that they had been unfairly maligned by the media.[15] Kevin responded for the Louds on *The Dick Cavett Show*: "We don't say 'homo.' . . . That's what the newspapers say. We don't say it."

The advertising campaign gave clues of events to come, enticing audiences to stay with the program. The February 15 *New York Times* ad teased, "Next week problems between the couple begin to reveal themselves, and their son Grant has a car accident. The following week Pat decides to file for divorce. Follow the drama of TV's first real family." Later advertisements were less sensational, conceivably even in response to criticisms of earlier ones. The January 25 ad in the *New York Times* tried to provide some balance: "Conflict and strain are showing between them, but you'll see some of the positive aspects of their marriage: cooperation when a special problem arises, and shared pride in their daughters. Conflict, cooperation and pride. Aren't they part of most families?" More in keeping with the title, later advertising portrayed the family as basically similar to everyone else.

By February 1, 1973, the advertising campaign included quotes from reviews that had appeared in the *New York Times, Harper's, TV Guide, Cue, Vogue,* and the *Saturday Review of the Arts.* The February 8 ad in the *New York Times* stated, "*Newsweek* described this series as 'a starkly intimate portrait of one family struggling to survive a private civil war.' See for yourself." The WNET publicity campaign lent an aura of sensationalism to *An American Family* and a certain freakish nature to the Louds. The producers themselves were dissatisfied with the advertisements. (Station personnel put the ads together in association with an independent firm owned by Lawrence Grossman, who was later to be president of PBS.) "We were crazed by them, but you can't control everything in this field," associate producer Susan Lester confessed. "You might see a promo and get a twinge. It's not exactly what you want, but if you fight everything then you have no credibility. You have to pick your battles." At a 1988 Museum of Broadcasting seminar on the series, Susan Raymond disagreed: "As a producer, you have a responsibility from the beginning to the end of a show to get it through the publicity mill." When Pat Loud complained to Craig Gilbert about the advertisements, he replied that promotion was out of his control.[16] Although the producer claimed he was not responsible for the WNET campaign, which he later referred to as "inaccurate, misleading, and highly exploitive," some of the copy came from his 1971 proposal.[17]

Gilbert paid a heavy price for the crass publicity. Although many aspects of the program tagged it as a serious educational documentary, there were contradictory signals. The blend of seriousness and sensationalism that greeted the series issued from the combination of a "highbrow" (documentary) mode with "lowbrow" (situation comedy and soap opera) ones. References to the series as a soap opera invariably carried negative associations of melodrama and triviality. The press packet brought together Margaret Mead and *Father Knows Best.* Coming at a time when TV was still a popular medium derided by most intellectuals, this explosive mixture explains why magazines like *The Nation* viciously denounced the documentary and why a critic for the *Village Voice* concluded, "If this were a sane civilization, it would be a ridiculous show."[18]

Articles in the national press set the tone for critical responses in the following months, often being quoted in other reviews as well as in advertisements. Early articles were probably based on the press portfolio, a screening of several shows—particularly episode one—and, in some cases, interviews with the production team. When the first reviews appeared, the series was not even finished; programs nine, ten, eleven, and twelve remained in the editing stage. Craig Gilbert still hoped to extend the documentary to fifteen shows to make it "a logical whole."[19] The roll call of material wealth, lifted verbatim from the press release, cropped up in many reviews. Stephanie Harrington, writing in the *New York Times,* surmised that the Louds found in Santa Barbara "their approximation of the American Dream—an eight-room ranch house, a horse, three dogs, a pool, a Jaguar, a Volvo, a Toyota, and a Datsun pickup."[20] The press packet simplified the reviewing process; critics would have had difficulty piecing together such a string of possessions just by watching the twelve episodes. Indeed, the absence of this kind of quantitative detail remains one of the principal weaknesses of the observational style. The press release established the Louds as wealthy but discontented Californians, the inverse of the poor but virtuous Waltons of Virginia.

▶

The Neighbors Next Door

Most reviewers of *An American Family* failed to recognize the mediation involved and talked about the Louds as if they were their next-door neighbors. Anecdotal evidence suggests that ordinary viewers did this to an even greater extent than professional critics. Many reviewers saw *An American Family* as the high point of film and television realism. Reviewer Gail Rock contended in *Ms.* that the show was "more candid than Allen Funt's wildest dreams."[21] Literary critic Roger Rosenblatt, writing in the *New Republic,* concurred: "Never was there greater realism on television except in the murders of Oswald and Robert Kennedy."[22] One striking development—

BERRY'S WORLD

© 1973 by NEA, Inc.

Jim Berry

*"FIRST I suggest that we try to cope with your own family
—THEN we can try to cope with the Loud family!"*

The cartoon *Berry's World* captures popular reactions to *An American Family. Berry's World* reprinted by permission of Newspaper Enterprise Association, Inc.

the climax of the reality effect—was the belief that the Louds had lived their lives on television and that television was absorbing the real. In *Commonweal*, theater director Michael Murray asked, "What is it like to live on television?" and the first review in the *New York Times* was titled "*An American Family* Lives Its Life on TV."[23]

All documentaries invite referential readings, and they were by far the most common responses to *An American Family*. In this instance, viewers "relate to characters as real people and in turn relate these real people to their own real worlds."[24] Most reviewers speculated at length about the Louds. A comment offered by Shana Alexander in *Newsweek* was typical: "At school, at home, at work and at play, these nice-looking people act like affluent zombies. The shopping carts overflow, but their minds are empty."[25] For Alexander, the documentary provided not only a window into the Louds' ranch house, but a view into their innermost thoughts, or lack thereof. By taking the program as a transparent representation, most reviewers effectively attributed authorship to the Louds. Anne Roiphe's nine-page article in the *New York Times Magazine*—the longest published response while the broadcast was in progress—was really about the Louds, hardly about the series at all. Roiphe brought a novelist's imagination to her review. Of Mr. Loud's extramarital affairs, she speculated, "Why the infidelities? The camera doesn't tell us, but we can guess."[26]

Reviewers, regardless of whether they believed the family was representative, attacked the Louds for all kinds of personal shortcomings. Few found points in common with the family. In some instances, these criticisms reached absurd proportions, as in Roiphe's censure of the fifteen-year-old Delilah, who "never grieved for the migrant workers, the lettuce pickers, the war dead; never thought of philosophy or poetry, was not obsessed by adolescent idealism, did not seem undone by dark moods in which she pondered the meaning of life and death."[27] Although semiologist Sol Worth once pointed out that "pictures can't say ain't," Roiphe based her conjectures about Delilah entirely on the *absence* of certain scenes in *An American Family*.[28]

Roiphe reserved her most vicious comments for Lance, expressing shock at his "flamboyant, leechlike, homosexuality."[29] Her homophobia did not go unchallenged; a letter to the editor of the *New York Times* from the president of the Gay Activists Alliance came to the defense of Lance and his family.[30] Three months later, members of the GAA met with representa-

Delilah Loud in *An American Family*.

tives of the Association of Motion Picture and Television Producers to protest the depiction of gays and lesbians in commercial film and TV, marking the beginning of a gradual transformation in American media.[31] Roiphe epitomized the many elite magazine reviewers, themselves novelists and cultural critics, who disliked the Louds. Her remarkable essay ended with the nostalgic wish that the country could "return to an earlier America when society surrounded its members with a tight sense of belonging," a feeling that Roiphe found in *The Waltons* (1972–81), which she reviewed nine months later in the same magazine.[32] Roiphe engaged in the same imaginative projection—asking herself, "What kind of America do I want to live in?"—with the documentary series as with the fictional one.

▶

The Medium Frames the Message

An American Family provided a framework for people to think about their lives. The open-ended episodic structure of the program, broadcast weekly, accentuated similarities with everyday life and promoted strong identification with the Louds. The twelve-part series powerfully combined the reality effect of soap opera narrative with documentary conventions of authenticity. The production secretary underlined the bond fostered between viewers and the Louds. "I think when one watched *An American Family*," Alice Carey recalled, "one knew that somewhere in Santa Barbara *they* were watching the same thing."

The notion of liveness, a characteristic dimension of television viewing, cropped up in plenty of the reviews. Many critics failed to make distinctions between representation and reality. An article in *Newsweek* announced, "This week, in the presence of 10 million Americans, Pat Loud will tell her husband of twenty years to move out of their house in Santa Barbara, Calif."[33] By the time the series was broadcast, Bill and Pat had already divorced. Like many others, this review collapsed the difference between story time and broadcast time, implying that viewers saw the events not as they had happened, but as they were happening. Given this predisposition, it is no wonder critics accused the Louds of exhibitionism. Whereas the family experienced the shooting as an intimate affair—"it's just that Susan and Alan were in the room," in Lance's words—reviewers experienced the broadcast as part of a national audience.

The medium of television greatly influenced reactions to *An American Family*. Media scholar John Ellis sees the liveness effect as one of its essential features: "The broadcast TV image has the effect of immediacy. It is as though the TV image is a 'live' image, transmitted and received in the same moment that it is produced."[34] Clearly, in 1973, reviewers associated *An American Family* not only with the real world but with the simultaneity of the live broadcast. Surely such comments would not have occurred if, like the Maysles brothers' *Salesman* (1969), Gilbert's documentary had been shown in movie theaters.

A further consequence of the role of television concerns the relationships among entertainment, reality, and broadcasting in the 1970s. Some critics saw the Louds' willingness to share their private lives in a TV program as representative of a therapeutic society thriving on a "compulsion to confess," an indication of the weakening of America's moral fiber.[35] Writing in the April 1979 issue of the *New Republic,* film critic Stanley Kauffmann counted this compulsion as the principal, inadvertent, sociological insight of *An American Family.*[36] With this in mind, reviewers in *The Nation* and *Time* attacked the Louds for appearing in the documentary. For these critics, the Louds were not only "affluent zombies," they were doubly fools for allowing a film crew into their home. Accusations of invasion of privacy on the part of the producers and exhibitionism on the part of the family led to the denunciation of television.[37] Critics took the show as a sign of a society increasingly based on spectacle; indeed, some reviewers perceived the Louds as a family *invented* by the media. Sara Sanborn contended in *Commentary,* "Lance seems to have been literally brought to life by television; it is hard to believe that he exists when no one is watching."[38] Just the *idea* of the show was taken as a symptom of moral decline. The low critical status of TV plagued the series, confirming Bruce Gronbeck's observation that much television criticism functions to proclaim the worthlessness of the medium.[39]

Hostility toward TV led some reviewers to speculate about television swallowing the real, anticipating postmodernist theories. "A delightful only-in-America scenario presents itself: will the Louds eventually appear on TV," Crawford Woods mused, "to promote the book they'll write about having been on TV?"[40] Once again, the medium was the message; Allan King's *A Married Couple* (1969), which inspired *An American Family,* did not lead to denunciations of cinema. Critics envisioned various paranoid scenarios of the encroachment of television in everyday life. Michael Murray, a freelance writer and theater director, imagined a black hole of programming devoted to the series: "TV critics will become involved in broadcast debates with the Louds and will thus themselves become participants in the drama. Margaret Mead herself may be sucked in, explaining her anthropological interpretations to Pat and Bill on TV and then, as they react to her theories, becoming inexorably a part of what she is analyzing."[41] Such critics saw nonfiction TV as a dangerous, shadowy substitute for reality.

Suddenly, with *An American Family,* television became a postmodern hall of mirrors. Presumably, as far as these reviewers were concerned, Americans would have been better off if TV remained simply a medium of fantasy and escape. Gilbert certainly did not want to be on the receiving end of commentary on the detrimental role of the media, especially given that his program was conceived as a revisionist depiction of family life. Although the producer would undoubtedly agree that television obscures social relations, his series was designed to *critique* this aspect of the medium, not exemplify it. Highbrow TV reviewers simply failed to recognize that they had an ally in Craig Gilbert. Consider how the producer's intentions backfired in Stephanie Harrington's assessment; she wrote in *The Nation,* "The television series and the Louds' freakish celebrity, for which they have paid a painful price, contribute to an analysis of our cultural condition only by adding to the pile of familiar symptoms."[42] Broadcast on television, *An American Family* became part of the problem. In the battle between television and "a real view of middle-class life," TV won.

This perspective came full circle when the Louds themselves started to maintain that television undermined traditional family values and exacerbated the generation gap. In an article first published in February 1973, Pat invoked the argument that TV is a drug: "As a parent, I've been battling television for years. . . . Will it turn the kids into addict-observers, career spectators rather than participants?"[43] One year after *An American Family* was aired, Bill Loud criticized TV for undermining the work ethic: "If I had to do it all over again I'd beat hell out of those kids and throw their goddamn television sets into the Pacific. TV gave them a completely unreal picture of the world."[44] For all involved, television became a convenient scapegoat for perceived breakdowns of American culture.

Referential readings, focused on the seven Louds, were the most prevalent responses to *An American Family.* They were, of course, counseled by WNET's press materials and advertisements that insisted that the program was "actually lived by the Loud family of California." (Still today, when I give lectures about the series, someone always asks about what happened to Pat, Bill, Lance, Kevin, Grant, Delilah, and Michele Loud. Few ask about Gilbert, the Raymonds, or NET.) In addition, newspaper and magazine reviewers asserted that the Louds had "lived their lives on television," thereby perverting boundaries between TV and everyday life.

The End of the American Dream

Despite reviewers' profound dependence on the publicity campaign, quite a few of the articles about the series went beyond simple summaries of the press materials. Many critics had other public identities, especially feminist authors such as anthropologist Margaret Mead, who had just published her autobiography *Blackberry Winter;* journalist Shana Alexander, author of *The Feminine Eye* and, later, of the *State-by-State Guide to Women's Legal Rights;* Anne Roiphe, whose 1970 novel *Up the Sandbox!* examined a struggling marriage from the perspective of a young mother; and Abigail McCarthy, whose autobiography *Private Faces/Public Places* chronicled her life with her husband, politician Eugene McCarthy.[45] Some reviewers resisted the interpretive frames offered by WNET. For example, *Newsweek* and *Time* explicitly challenged the issue of the representativeness of the Louds, which was heavily accented in the press packet. *The Nation* offered a point-for-point rebuttal of the press materials, noting that Gilbert had "an exaggerated admiration for the analytical powers of his medium and a doleful view of the homogeneity of American life."[46]

Many compared the series to fictional forms, and others contested the impression of reality that the series offered. The linguist S. I. Hayakawa claimed that it was "a most artificial situation," and an anonymous reviewer in *The Nation* concluded that "the mirror is false."[47] By abandoning traditional conventions of nonfiction, Gilbert's documentary undermined its own believability with a segment of the American television audience. The "neither fish nor fowl" generic instability of the series was one of its most striking aspects. "Producers, writers, directors, distributors, and exhibitors index their films as nonfiction," Noël Carroll has argued. "We don't characteristically go to films about which we must guess whether they are fiction or nonfiction. They are generally indexed one way or the other."[48] But from the very outset, *An American Family* bridged this divide, calling to mind soap operas, situation comedies, and documentaries. It blended the narrative and rhetorical modes of viewer engagement typically offered by American TV. To borrow from Robert Allen's description of soap operas, to a greater extent than any other documentary, Gilbert's series walked the line between a program that "spills over into the experiential world of the viewer" and a program that may be "read as fiction."[49] Critics compared it to home movies, television commercials, talk shows, variety shows, situation comedies, soap operas, novels, plays, sociological studies, and documentaries.

Going beyond speculation about the Louds themselves, these reviewers paid particular attention to narrative conventions, the point of view of the documentary, and the making of the series. Looking for generic comparisons, critics cast about for terms to describe the twelve-part show adequately. References to *An American Family* as a "home movie" typically served to discredit the program, home movies being regarded as banal and of interest only to their subjects.[50] Several reviewers commented that the Louds seemed to step right out of the sanitized world of TV commercials.[51] Erica Brown concluded in *Vogue,* "The manufacturer of Barbie dolls could not have typecast a family better."[52]

Few critics compared *An American Family* to sociological studies of the family, although the WNET press materials quoted Margaret Mead and cited the work of Oscar Lewis.[53] Of course, television critics were not qualified to cite sociological research. (Given their reliance on the press portfolio, many were barely equipped to discuss the program in relation to TV shows.) Journalists did, however, use the series as a springboard to write about family life generally.[54] *Time* magazine solicited comments from a psychotherapist, a psychologist, a psychiatrist, and two sociologists.[55] A roundtable discussion broadcast by WNET on April 5, a week after the final episode aired and in the same weekly time slot as the show, featured the opinions of Mead and a panel of scholarly experts on literature, drama, history, psychiatry, and anthropology. The variety of disciplines represented on the panel demonstrated the difficulty reviewers had fitting Gilbert's series to established genres and forms.

Virtually the only tradition to which the program was not compared was nonfiction film. The WNET press packet simply noted that *An American Family* was *not* a "survey type of documentary."[56] Taking their cues from the publicity campaign, most reviewers did not mention other nonfiction programs. Almost none cited the history of observational cinema; this was the first time the style reached a mass audience. A few critics, looking for nonfictional comparisons, mentioned such works as *The Selling of the Pentagon, 60 Minutes,* and *Titicut Follies.*[57] A reviewer in the *Chicago Tribune* suggested that the program was "a sort of non-fiction novel."[58] Surprisingly, no one mentioned the Maysles brothers' *Salesman,* which playwright Arthur Miller had referred to as "an adventure into the American dream."[59]

Not surprisingly, reviewers writing for specialized film magazines cited nonfiction precedents with greater frequency. Writing in *Media and Methods,* educator Robert Geller referred to the films of the Maysleses, Wiseman, King, and Arthur Barron.[60] But the narrative basis of the series, combined with a lack of familiarity with observational cinema, led most critics to other forms. Again, the *New York Times* followed the suggestion of the press materials: "Unlike most documentaries, *An American Family* does not proceed from a premise and then marshal the evidence to dramatize that premise."[61] Traditional documentary style was invoked only in contrast to the singularity of Gilbert's program.

Critical readers believed that the show had as much in common with fictional forms as with the documentary tradition. O'Connor referred to the hybrid series as a "sad comedy."[62] Others compared it to soap operas. For many, the interest of *An American Family* came from the novelty of seeing the intimate life of an actual family portrayed in serial form: "You find yourself sticking with the Louds with the same compulsion that draws you back day after day to your favorite soap opera. The tension is heightened by the realization that you are identifying, not with a fictitious character, but a flesh and blood person who is responding to personal problems of the kind you yourself might face."[63] In between episodes, viewers had time to speculate with friends about family members and story developments to come. The serial form, coupled with the focus on intimate family life, encouraged an unusually intense level of interest in the Louds. They received substantial amounts of mail from fans, as do many actors who portray fictional characters on daytime serials.

More thoughtful reviewers, those with more time and space to develop their ideas, called attention to the principles of selection of *An American Family*. These critics discussed the series as a "construction with aesthetic rules."[64] This perspective engendered nagging doubts about the program's status as nonfiction. Some had difficulty reconciling the story emphasis with the actuality material, as if documentary were, by definition, a nonnarrative form. Jim Gaines noted in the *Saturday Review of the Arts* that the "most striking narrative moments seem to conspire against seeing the film as true-to-life," a comment that suggests tightly organized stories must be fictional.[65] Clearly, the narrative drive of the show grated against the realism of the handheld camera and direct sound. Gaines found it implausible that a tarot card reader in episode two accurately hinted at Pat's coming separation from Bill.[66] Indeed, the scene strongly forecasts later plot developments, as the card reader suggests to Pat, "This year is a year of changes. You'll have a choice to make which you are building up to. Something is ending now." *Newsweek* speculated that "their impromptu remarks seem improbably articulate, as though they had been scripted ahead of time."[67] Use of continuity editing techniques, suspense, and foreshadowing lent a fictional tone to the series. Reviewers neglected to consider that the editors put the documentary together retrospectively, with the divorce in mind. Looking over seven months of footage, the editors had the power the tarot reader lacked, to predict the future accurately.

Because the program was edited does not mean that it was fiction, nor does the fact that *An American Family* told stories mean that it was a fabrication. For some reviewers, however, the narrative thrust of documentary undermined the reality effect. In *The Classical Hollywood Cinema*, film historian David Bordwell suggests that "the strongest illusion of reality comes from tight causal motivation."[68] Viewers find Hollywood films believable if all the threads of their stories are tightly sewn up; realism derives from narrative coherence. Reactions to Gilbert's series suggest just the opposite about nonfiction; if things fit together too neatly, viewers distrust the narration and question the realism.

The narrative drive of *An American Family* influenced its reception in other ways. Stories require change from one state of affairs to another. The Louds' separation provided narrative momentum; some critics attributed this change to the presence of the crew. Pat, for her part, maintained that she and Bill stayed together *longer* than they otherwise would have.[69] In his letter to Lance read in voice-over in episode eleven, Bill speaks of wanting a new life for himself that he had "considered for some time." He later confirmed that the decision to separate had nothing to do with the filming. Similarly, reviewers typically stated that Lance "came out of the closet" during production, attributing this, too, to the camera's presence. Lance replied that he was gay before, during, and after the shooting. "The sexual preference has always been there," he told the *Chicago Tribune*. "When I went thru puberty, I wanted to have sex with boys."[70]

Given the predisposition of the critics, any narrative development—apart from natural disasters, presumably—was bound to be attributed to the presence of the camera. Change, by definition, would be caused by the crew, so if Delilah had decided to marry her boyfriend, or Kevin had enrolled in the military, or Grant had run away from home, reviewers would have speculated that the filming provoked those events. The narrative drive of the documentary inadvertently positioned the camera as cause and the Louds' actions as effects.

Critical readers—those predisposed to look for stylistic conventions, messages, and authors—were not obliged to reference fiction. They could have related the show to the evolution of film and television documentary, the different nonfiction modes Bill Nichols mentions in his 1983 article "The Voice of Documentary"—Griersonian direct address, observational, interview, and reflexive—or the work of such well-known auteurs as Robert Flaherty (*Nanook of the North*, 1922).[71] The novel subject matter of Gilbert's program, however, fostered associations with fiction. As film scholar Colin Young noted, "Series like *An American Family* are beginning to deal with a level of intimate behavior that till now has been the province of fiction."[72]

Throughout their articles, reviewers compared the series to a variety of mostly fictional television shows, movies, novels, and plays, including *The Waltons, Father Knows Best, The Partridge Family, Who's Afraid of Virginia Woolf?, Scenes from a Marriage, A Doll's House,* and *Death of a Salesman.* Some critics invoked these fictional works, especially situation comedies, for contrast—for example, "no *Ozzie and Harriet* confection," "a lot more fun than *Peyton Place,*" and "scarcely *The Forsyte Saga* it is billed to be."[73] For some, *An American Family* offered a corrective to idealized fictional representations: "The reality of the Louds has no connection with the fantasy of *The Brady Bunch.*"[74] In this light, *An American Family* may be more effective as a critique of family life on fictional television than as a statement about contemporary American society.

Although most reviewers focused relentlessly on the personalities of the family members, others intuited that the Louds stood for more than themselves, as in Shana Alexander's comment that the documentary depicted a "genuine American tragedy."[75] Some recognized that the program had a purpose beyond simply showing life at 35 Wooddale Lane. These critics took *An American Family* as a statement about contemporary society, supporting Bill Nichols's claim that documentaries are films that make arguments. Reviewers who interpreted the series as a commentary on American culture also tended to identify the producer as the source. For example, short plot summaries in *TV Guide* attributed authorship to Gilbert—for example, "Producer Craig Gilbert hints how the family's summer separation may have deeper roots."[76] Although most critics did *not* read *An American Family* as an argument, some definitely did.

In thematic terms, critical readers asserted that the documentary offered "a scathing commentary on the American domestic dream," made "a statement about the values of marriage and family," and chronicled "the American Dream turned nightmare."[77] Reviewers did not interpret the Louds' separation as a positive step toward ending an unhappy marriage or as a message, for example, of liberation. They favored Gilbert's perspective on the divorce over that of the Louds. Furthermore, the program documented "the erosion of traditional values," "the generation gap," the inability "to communicate," spiritual emptiness, and "conspicuous consumption."[78] In the words of anthropologist Gloria Levitas, the series chronicled the disappearance of "a central core of belief."[79] According to Abigail McCarthy, writing in the *Atlantic,* the Loud family stood as "a symbol of disintegration and purposelessness in American life."[80] A letter to the editor of the *New York Times Magazine* summed up many responses by quoting Thomas Jefferson: "Material abundance without character is the surest way to destruction."[81] The Louds did not manage to come across as the "West Coast Kennedys," as Bill had anticipated.[82] The dominant interpretation of the series was that it chronicled the breakdown of American culture; the center, Robert Geller noted, quoting Didion quoting Yeats, would no longer "hold."[83]

Under other circumstances, such a show might not have been controversial at all. In 1976, the public television series *Six American Families* provoked no controversy whatsoever although it explored the farm crisis, the generation gap, divorce, religion, ethnicity, gender, racism, and poverty in the United States. Attitudes about marriage, homosexuality, and women's liberation in 1973 combined with an unconventional style to make *An American Family* unusually provocative. Moreover, a new threshold of private disclosure was crossed. The program tapped into a general pessimism about the country in the 1970s, concerning divorce and the family, materialism and the absence of community, the decline of traditional values, and the detrimental role of television.

The documentary played into fears about the collapse of the United States, which became particularly acute with the end of the postwar boom in 1973. "Notions about the decline of the American family became entangled with notions about the decline of the American character, which in turn became entangled with notions of the decline of the economy and of the American empire."[84] Rupert Wilkinson identified this trend in writing on American social character of the period, including the fears of "falling apart" and of "falling away from the standards of the past."[85] Like other social critics, Craig Gilbert tried to say that the American dream had become, in Charles Reich's words in *The Greening of America,* "a rags-to-riches type of narrow materialism."[86] *An American Family* made this perspective available to a TV audience, critiquing the modern consumer society at a turning point from expansion to contraction.

The Louds appeared on the March 12, 1973, cover of *Newsweek;* the issue included a series of articles devoted to divorce and the American family. The magazine cover showed a smiling family portrait with a mocking title, "The Broken Family." Set against the tranquil family life of *The Adventures of Ozzie & Harriet,* Bill and Pat's separation stood out as a catastrophe, although Delilah, for her part, told *Newsweek* that she considered the divorce "a relief."[87] By establishing the "American dream" as the point of comparison in the press materials and the series, Gilbert succeeded in making the fall of the family greater; he raised the stakes to the level of tragedy. (In this light, a gay son in such a family could only have been a "nightmare.") Pat Loud tried to contradict this response, maintaining that her family "demonstrated that divorce is not tragic failure."[88]

Many reviewers, such as Roiphe and Geller, bemoaned the fact that the Louds did not live up to the tragic implications of the divorce, that they did not conduct themselves with the larger-than-life stature of the characters in Arthur Miller's *Death of a Salesman* or Henrik Ibsen's *A Doll's House*. These critics missed the histrionics, the poignancy, and the catharsis of great theater. "No Rachel or King Lear crying for their kids. No Willie Loman blathering in the victory garden."[89] Reviewers craved the sharp emotional clarity of fiction—in which every scene and every shot reveals character—the model many brought with them to understand the program. Echoing Geller's comments, Michael Murray, founder of the Charles Playhouse in Boston, complained in *Commonweal* of the Louds' failure to reveal themselves: "None of these griefs is ever expressed directly."[90] Novelist Roiphe opted for fiction over documentary, concluding her review with a reference to Francis Ford Coppola's *The Godfather* (1972): "Maybe it's better to be a Corleone than a Loud."[91]

Expectations from fiction film and television conditioned many responses. Because the Louds did not have strongly articulated goals toward which they were striving, goals found in protagonists of classical Hollywood narratives and even in such early Drew Associates films as *Primary* (1960) and *On the Pole* (1960), reviewers found their actions aimless and without meaning. Nor did the family members have the facility of characters on daytime TV serials to articulate their feelings. Amherst English professor Benjamin DeMott faulted *An American Family* for failing to disclose the "crucial inner speech" of the Louds, such as a "great novel" would have.[92] Gilbert later acknowledged the insufficiency of the observational style when he wrote, "The series conveyed a good idea of what the Louds were doing, [but] it didn't convey very much at all about what they were thinking."[93] The absence of clearly articulated desires—such as becoming a rock star, getting into UCLA, learning a foreign language—led reviewers to see the Loud family as "a symbol of disintegration and purposelessness." At least one critic, John W. Donohue, a Catholic priest and associate editor of *America,* attributed this absence to the limitations of the observational approach: "One learned nothing significant about the Louds' history or their present relationship to their times."[94]

There were critics who agreed that *An American Family* made an argument about the demise of American culture, but who questioned the evidence the show provided. During a roundtable talk show broadcast on WNET, Rutgers University anthropologist Lionel Tiger accused Gilbert of having a "profound prejudice" against American family life.[95] Sociologists were quick to note that the family constituted a "sample of one," as an article in *Time* asserted.[96] Reviewers argued that the Louds were not statistically representative, nor could any one family adequately portray the diversity of American life.[97] In a strange twist, critics maintained that participating in the program placed the Louds outside the mainstream of American life, that they were closet exhibitionists. Sociologist Irving Horowitz claimed, "The very act of being filmed for public television makes the Louds untypical."[98] *Newsweek* paraphrased Horowitz's reasoning for the conclusion to its cover story on the documentary: "The minute Craig Gilbert's cameras began to roll in May 1971, the Loud family became anything but typical."[99]

Arguments imply evidence, but the Loud family offered just a single instance. These sociologists preferred to see the family as an idiosyncratic case, rather than as a symbolic representation, and, as a result, searched for ways to dismiss the Louds, to make them "untypical." Horowitz's self-defeating argument was simply a reaction to the novelty of the documentary approach. Would he have said that the very act of answering a survey questionnaire makes the Louds untypical? Typicality itself is a sociological construct based on statistical methods; the Bunkers of *All in the Family* were not statistically representative either. The Louds were not typical; they were, in University of Virginia historian Joseph Kett's view, "archetypical."[100]

▶ ───

The Presence of the Camera

> *The reason I think so many people are talking about this program is not only that it touches on real people's lives, but it has made a lot of people aware of the fact that in a television show there is an interaction between filmer and subject.*
> :: S. I. Hayakawa, *Chicago Tribune*, March 11, 1973

The single most distinctive characteristic of the reception of *An American Family* was the critics' obsession with the making of the documentary, unprecedented in the history of the form. Reviewers eventually became more preoccupied with how the program was made than with what it said or meant. A vocal minority challenged the basic presuppositions of observational cinema, especially the influence of the camera on family interactions.

Many articles discussed the making of the program: the duration of the shoot, the number of hours recorded, the rapport with the family, the motivations of the producer and the Louds, and the influence of the camera. As S. I. Hayakawa correctly noted, the series "made a lot of people aware of the fact that in a television show there is an interaction between filmer and subject."[101] Some articles were devoted exclusively to providing the backstage details of the production, such as one headlined "Looking thru the Lens at One Man's Family" in the *Chicago Tribune*.[102] An entire episode of *The Dick Cavett Show* explored the making of the documentary.

So much speculation was devoted to details of the production that TV critic John J. O'Connor complained in the *New York Times,* "The content of *An American Family* slowly began sinking into a mindless ooze about the making of *An American Family*."[103] During the ensuing controversy, the producer made more explicit claims about his point of view. "We were not trying to re-create seven months in this family's life," Gilbert admitted. "We were using the film to say something about this country and what it means to be a man and a woman. The divorce was simply used as a dramatic device."[104] Gilbert acknowledged that Ross Macdonald's detective novel *The Underground Man* described "with absolute accuracy the kind of family I was looking for," a revealing detail not provided in the press packet.[105] Television critics expressed disappointment that the producer had a point of view.[106]

Reviewers had a right to be disappointed, given Gilbert's hands-off stance in the publicity materials. The program depended on the impression that the series transparently reproduced the everyday lives of the Louds. Gilbert took a producing credit rather than a directing credit—a decision that he would eventually regret—because he did not want to undermine viewers' inclinations to read the program as, he later wrote, "a recording of real life as it happened."[107] *An American Family,* like all documentaries, embodies tensions between interpretation and record. Gilbert owned up to this fact when he said years later that producers of nonfiction use human beings "to make a point."[108]

Review after review of *An American Family* discovered that documentaries were not natural events, but the product of human intervention. "Craig Gilbert, the producer, is there. He is now an essential part of the drama. Not only has the *New York Times* linked him to Pat, but now the whole family angrily wants to know why he took out one sequence and left in another. He stutters and stumbles. The audience is getting its first glimpse of this character who has been so much a part of the process."[109] Paradoxically, the more documentary producers remove conventional traces of authorial presence—such as on-camera narrators, voice-over narration, scored music, and interviews—the more problematic their influence becomes.

Reviews accentuated the backstage details that the program itself kept in the shadows. Melinda Ward wrote in *Film Comment,* "The audience knows, especially after all the publicity, how long the crew was there, how many hours were shot, etc."[110] Many believed that the production of the series held clues to its legitimacy as a representation. Rather than accepting that the show commented on contemporary society, many reasoned that any point of view meant bias. Following this line of reasoning, reviewers focused on the making of the documentary—for example, the editing—to discover where it went wrong, where the holy grail of objectivity was lost. *An American Family* may be best remembered as a nonfiction program *haunted by the presence of the camera,* an unwittingly reflexive work, even though Gilbert tried to make "a series of films about the Louds and not about how the Louds interrelated with a film crew."[111]

Rare was the review that did not speculate about the influence of the camera on the family, exemplified by an anonymous reviewer's comment in *America,* "As this journal of deterioration unfolds, one must ask continually: 'Might it have been otherwise if there were no camera and no microphone?'"[112] Writing in the *Chicago Tribune,* S. I. Hayakawa, then president of San Francisco State College, pointedly asked, "Can a documentary be made of real life?"[113] His answer was no. Reviewers who called attention to the presence of the camera usually dismissed the *idea* of observational cinema rather than mentioning specific examples from the series. To buttress their arguments, they paraphrased physicist Werner Heisenberg's principle of indeterminacy to challenge the notion of simple observation. Critic (and, later, novelist) Daniel Menaker, a *New Yorker* editor writing in *Harper's,* submitted that "the *process* of conducting certain kinds of experiments alters the very *properties* under investigation."[114] A reviewer in *The Nation* contended that "intervention in the life of a social microcosm significantly changes the phenomena under observation," and Crawford Woods, writing in the *New Republic,* maintained that "the observer is never wholly independent of the observed."[115] Sara Sanborn took this argument to its logical conclusion in *Commentary,* arguing that "the medium has created the phenomenon it now purports to study."[116] Others, such as Cavett and Hayakawa, cited their own, admittedly nonscientific, experiences of being filmed as proof of the intrusiveness of the camera.[117]

Not surprisingly, the Heisenberg argument was one of the highbrow responses to the program, something reviewers never bothered to mention about traditional documentaries, television news, nonfiction writing, sociological studies, or journalism, all forms in which the conventions were more or less taken for granted. Hayakawa suggested in the *Chicago Tribune* that *An American Family* was "a most artificial situation." Are we to assume that *The Dick Cavett Show* and *60 Minutes* are not? Although Heisenberg's principle announced a profound relativism, critics brought it up not because they shared the radicalism of Heisenberg's insight, but because they desired objectivity. Gilbert is correct when he says that this use of the Heisenberg principle raises doubts "not only about *An American Family* but about all documentaries."[118]

These reviewers ignored comments from the Loud family that contradicted their arguments. The Louds noted that they gradually accepted the camera's presence. "'After some months the crew was like family,' explains Pat. 'I acted as if they were part of us. I just forgot about the camera.'"[119] Bill recalled the most controversial scene, in which his wife asked him to move out of the house: "When Patty told me about the divorce, I could have said, 'Get this camera crew out of here.' But we had gotten used to them."[120] Gilbert asked the Louds to behave "as if" the camera were not there, a conventional arrangement with which they more or less complied. Similarly, the producer asked the audience to watch the series "as if" the camera were not there; significant segments of the viewing public refused this gambit.

In their discussions of the making of the documentary, most critics focused on the shooting stage rather than on pre- or postproduction, underemphasizing the importance of both casting and editing. Postproduction came under scrutiny when the Louds maintained that the cutting betrayed their story. For some TV critics, the simple fact that the program was edited implied manipulation. They considered editing not a process of making meaning but rather a source of distortion and falsification.[121] Because reviewers assumed the purpose of the program was to reproduce the Louds'

Bill Loud on the phone in episode nine of *An American Family.*

experiences, trimming three hundred hours of film to twelve represented a betrayal. (Of course, from this perspective, the three hundred hours failed to preserve the thousands of hours lived during the filming, as others rushed to point out.) Given the footage, what else could Gilbert have done? Documentary filmmakers must select, condense, and create; as editor Dai Vaughan has noted, "The antithesis of the structured is not the truthful, or even the objective, but quite simply the random."[122] This was the producer's job.

[7] The Louds Strike Back

This series was the fulfillment of the middle-class dream that you can become famous for being just who you are.
:: Lance Loud[1]

A cartoon by William Hamilton, published in the March 17, 1973, issue of the *New Yorker,* while the series was still being broadcast, summed up many of the critical responses to *An American Family.* An elegant woman entertaining guests at dinner says, "I'm probably old-fashioned, but I felt much more at home with the Forsytes than with the Louds." Being a "symbol of disintegration and purposelessness in American life" was a heavy cross to bear. Stung by criticism of their lives, the Louds fought back and, in the process, became celebrities. Before the broadcast, their response to the documentary was positive. During the editing, family members viewed and gave their approval, both implicitly and explicitly, of the twelve episodes.[2] Pat wrote to the staff after one of the preview screenings, "You have eminently justified the faith my family tacitly put in you when we started this series."[3] Distraught over reactions to the program, the Louds accepted offers to appear on *The Mike Douglas Show* and *The Phil Donahue Show* to give their version of the filming. *Newsweek* reported that Lance was writing his own account of the making of the documentary.[4] Taking advantage of subsequent media exposure, the Louds became stars, in John Ellis's definition, "a performer in a particular medium whose figure enters into subsidiary forms of circulation, and then feeds back into future performances."[5]

Throughout the controversy, unlike the reviewers, the Louds directed attention toward the point of view of the series, especially the editing. They never denied having said and done the things that appear in *An American Family,* as occurred with some of the interviewees in *Hearts and Minds* (1974), Peter Davis's documentary about the American war in Vietnam. Although they claimed the documentary misrepresented their lives, they never implied that events were staged, accusations leveled against Jeff Kreines and Joel DeMott, the directors of *Seventeen* (1983).[6] Nor did the Louds maintain that they were performing or that the camera radically transformed their behavior. They simply asserted that the editors had a cynical view of American life. Responding to critics who harped on their inability to communicate, Pat accused Craig Gilbert of having "left out all the joyous, happy hours of communication and fun."[7] Bill claimed that the editors were New York radicals opposed to the traditional family and added, on *The Dick Cavett Show,* that given the opportunity to edit it themselves, they "would have done more of a *Laugh-In* type of thing."

The Louds tried to put out improved images of themselves. The premise of their appearance on the February 20, 1973, episode of *The Dick*

"I'm probably old-fashioned, but I felt much more at home with the Forsytes than I do with the Louds."

A cartoon about *An American Family* by William Hamilton, published in the *New Yorker.* Copyright The New Yorker Collection, 1973, William Hamilton from cartoonbank.com; all rights reserved.

Cavett Show was to give viewers a chance to meet the real Louds, not mediated by the series, as if the setting of the talk show were more believable than the scenes in *An American Family*. (It is astonishing how easily reviewers accepted this notion.) Cavett played up this contrast, finding the family "more likable in person than on television," something the Louds might also have said about him. Writing in the *Village Voice*, critic Sybil Carlin was content to note that she "felt more empathy" for the Loud family during the talk show than in the documentary.[8] Similarly, the *Chicago Tribune* published interviews with the family members in an article titled "Real-Life Louds Recall Their Days as TV's Louds," implying that television, unlike newspapers and magazines, distorts reality.[9] Subsequent representations of the family in the media promised glimpses of the Louds themselves, ironically standing the rhetorical claim of the observational style on its head. Many early observational films—such as *Primary* and *Don't Look Back*—subtly pointed out the ways in which the mass media construct actuality.[10]

By late February, the Louds' star status was fully confirmed. The *Chicago Tribune* devoted three articles to Bill and Lance's appearance on WLS-TV's *Kennedy and Co.* and *Kennedy at Night* programs: "The appearances were booked by their agent, a fellow named Jack Nakano, whose duties also include negotiating terms of books that both Bill and his ex-wife Pat are writing; of newspaper and magazine articles that various members of the family are writing; and also of the effort to get custody of all 300 hours of film that went into the public TV series."[11] Bill claimed during these appearances that his ex-wife received $150,000 for writing her autobiography. Reviewers took these actions as further evidence of the family's materialism. In a review of *Pat Loud: A Woman's Story*, Stephanie Harrington, who had lambasted *An American Family* in the *New York Times*, accused the Louds of turning their lives into "spectacle."[12]

Ironically, the Loud family swallowed the critics' appraisals of the series, just as the reviewers followed the lead of the press materials. In the *Chicago Tribune*, Bill even parroted the terms offered up by one critic: "We had a great family, really great people, a lot of ambitious people, and the children looked like affluent zombies looking into a pit."[13] They accepted the denigration of the series as soap opera; in Mr. Loud's words, "We let Gilbert and his crew into our house to do a documentary, and they produced a second-rate soap opera."[14] Once particular interpretations circulated, they were picked up by others with surprising consistency, from the producers and WNET personnel to reviewers and the Louds.

Every subsequent media exposure added to the growing portrait of the Louds, contesting *An American Family* at times, confirming it at others. The Los Angeles public TV station, KCET, auctioned "a weekend with the Louds" as part of a televised fund-raising event.[15] Unlike the celebrity of most performers, the Louds' star status emerged from their ongoing every-day lives, a fact that caused critical torment for reviewers. For stage director Michael Murray, the Louds were out of their genre: "Trying to write about it, however, is like reviewing a novel in which the characters spin on after the last page, popping up in the *Daily News* or on *The Dick Cavett Show* to demonstrate new attitudes, new characterizations and new hairstyles."[16]

In June 1973, the Warner Paperback Library, a division of Warner Books, Inc., published a printed version of *An American Family*. The book opened with Anne Roiphe's infamous essay from the February 18 issue of the *New York Times Magazine*, "Things Are Keen but Could Be Keener." It closed with Pat Loud's "Letter to *The Forum for Contemporary History*," in which she had the opportunity to respond to critics.[17] Sandwiched between these commentaries were transcripts of the twelve episodes with numerous photographs. The back cover roared, "NEVER BEFORE HAS TELEVISION PROBED SO CLOSE TO HUMAN TRUTH." Warner Paperback reportedly sold several hundred thousand copies.

The celebrity of the Louds continued well beyond the second national broadcast in the summer of 1973. Published in hardcover by Coward, McCann & Geoghegan, *Pat Loud: A Woman's Story* appeared in March 1974, one year after the airing of the documentary. Reviews of the book appeared in numerous publications, including *Cosmopolitan*, the *Library Journal*, the *Chicago Tribune*, the *New York Post*, the *Christian Science Monitor*, the *Los Angeles Times*, and *The Nation*. The autobiography, which Pat coauthored with freelance journalist Nora Johnson, sold well enough to merit a paperback printing by Bantam Books in December 1974.[18] As with Margaret Mead's autobiography, *Blackberry Winter*, the publicity capitalized on issues related to single motherhood, divorce, sexual liberation, and the women's movement. Sales figures for the book industry are hard to obtain, but the publisher organized an ambitious book tour for Pat Loud. During the promotional tour, she claimed to speak for the anonymous American wife and mother: "Every housewife I know has a story they are dying to tell but never do."[19] Fulfilling Crawford Woods's doomsday prediction, Pat Loud did appear on television to promote the book she wrote about appearing on TV. Literary critic Robert Kirsch, who

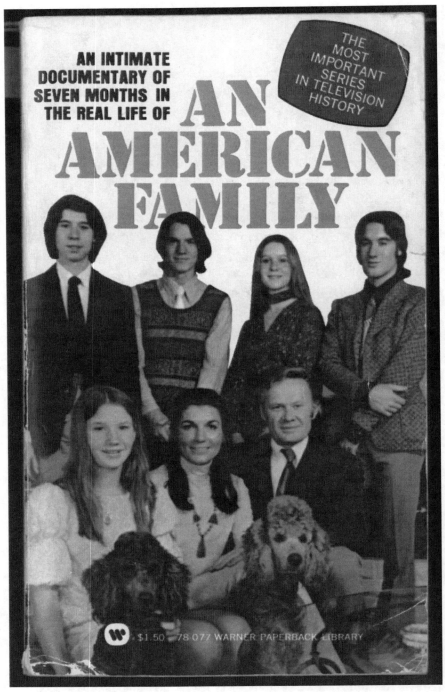

The cover of the book version of *An American Family*. Reprinted by permission of Warner Books, Inc.

had favorably reviewed Ross Macdonald's *The Underground Man* several years earlier, found Pat Loud's autobiography "worthy and even admirable" in a review published in the *Los Angeles Times*.[20]

The chapters on the Louds' participation in *An American Family* ("Why We Did It," "Living with a Camera Crew," and "What They Did—What They Said") offer the most remarkable testimony by the subject of a documentary in the history of the medium. Pat dedicates most of her prose to answering the critics, especially justifying her family's decision to take part in this experiment. Most viewers, seeing only the result of that pact on their home screens, could not imagine the steps that led to it. The Louds' biggest fault, to many reviewers, was simply the idiocy of participating in the project; presumably, any normal American family would have sent Gilbert packing. "Why We Did It" explains for inquiring minds who wanted to know, "There seem to be three groups of people—the ones like Craig, and Abigail McCarthy in *The Atlantic Monthly,* and I think me, who think *anybody* would have done it—the ones who think Californians would do it because they're exhibitionists and Easterners wouldn't because they're paranoid—and the ones who think *anybody* who would do it has got to be nuts, like Organized Psychiatry."[21]

Certain details in the autobiography suggest that Pat, too, came to view her life according to the commentary the program generated. She designates her family's arrival in Santa Barbara as "the American Dream."[22] The first chapter opens with comments that pick up where the series ended: "I still live in the house, but the pool is empty now," an off-the-cuff reference to Roiphe's designation of the Louds' swimming pool as a "fetid swamp."[23] This conspiracy of familiarity with the reader includes the disclosure of details of their ongoing lives. The book relies entirely on the notoriety of the television show, and Pat Loud's subsequent celebrity, as its raison d'être, assuming acquaintance with "TV's first real family."

Although documentaries occasionally turn their subjects into public personalities, fame for the Louds was not the inevitable result of their appearing in *An American Family*. The families featured on the PBS series *Six American Families* did not become stars. No one has ever gone on to become a celebrity from appearing in a film by Frederick Wiseman, although he has made more than thirty feature-length documentaries. Although a number of his films have engendered bitter controversy—especially *Titicut Follies, High School,* and *Primate*—they portray individuals in their social roles, not as personalities. Fully aware of his de-emphasis of individual characters, Wiseman maintains that "the star of each film is the institution."[24] Wiseman's dismantling of the traditional concept of character represents a reaction to earlier observational works as well as to the Hollywood star system. (Many classic verité films, such as *A Stravinsky Portrait, Don't Look Back,* and *Gimme Shelter,* focus on celebrities.) Quite deliberately, Wiseman's documentaries rarely identify characters by name. A review published in *Newsweek* nicely illustrates this fact: "[*Near Death* (1989) shows] how different doctors grapple with similar dilemmas in different ways. One—since he's never identified, let's call him Dr. Heart—envelops a patient's relatives with compassion."[25] In this brief article, the critic could not resist giving the character a name, although Wiseman's six-hour *Near Death* scrupulously avoids naming him.

An American Family, on the other hand, concentrated on the personalities of the family members and their daily activities. Furthermore, the serial broadcast encouraged ongoing viewer identification with the Louds over a span of several months. The WNET press packet facilitated identification with the individual characters through capsule biographies: "Fashionably dressed and casual in appearance, Pat Loud is an attractive brunette who looks younger than her 45 years."[26] Gilbert worked with some audience expectations (such as character-centered narrative) and against others (serial narrative in documentary, family life in nonfiction form). A comment from Abigail McCarthy in the *Atlantic* best expressed this audience response: "Their impact as individuals is what lingers in the viewer's memory."[27] In her autobiography, Pat mentions "boxes and boxes of letters" sent by viewers to the Louds.[28]

Some commentators saw a split between reviewers, who criticized the family severely, and ordinary viewers, whose responses were more sympathetic. Most of the mail the Louds received from viewers was considerate toward the family members. Brief citations in *Pat Loud: A Woman's Story* hint at some differences between ordinary viewers and professional critics. Letter writers did not relate *An American Family* to other works of art, such as plays and books, as reviewers tried to do. Ordinary viewers tended to compare their own personal experiences to those of the Louds. Pat summarizes the two thousand letters the family received: "Most of them said, We watched the series, we have a family like yours; don't pay any attention to the critics, hang tough."[29]

Many viewers wrote to the Louds after their first appearance on *The Dick Cavett Show,* during which Pat claimed that they had lost their "dignity" as a result of the documentary. "I really think most of them were written the very night of the Cavett show," she later noted. Many women identified strongly with Pat as a single mother: "If we decide to become women alone why must we explain to so many? Your private feelings for Lance are also nobody's damn business. Forsaking your child because he is not what you dreamed he would be is unthinkable. Many women admire you enormously on this point alone." Some wanted to assure Pat of her convictions. Others wished to discuss their own problems and how watching the documentary illuminated them: "One of the things women have always done was deprive themselves all their lives 'for the sake of their family' and to the detriment of themselves." Unlike the professional critics, these writers admitted their own faults. "I have also gotten drunk and regretted my words later. I bet 95 percent of the audience has, too." Some fulfilled Gilbert's hope that the series would be watched as a tool for self-analysis. "If I delve emotionally into your life it is more to understand myself and those around me than to criticize you." Still others offered advice. "Stay and keep the family . . . most men will come home and rock after a few flings."[30]

The letter writers did not maintain that the Louds made a mistake taking part in the program. Most expressed solidarity with Pat's situation as a woman, a former housewife, a divorcée, and a mother of five. To some extent the letters signal the nascence of a mass feminist consciousness. Clearly, Pat's character in the documentary was widely used as a foil to discuss general issues related to the women's movement. Surprisingly, these issues surfaced little in the published reviews of *An American Family;* only *Ms.* made any direct reference to women's liberation.[31] A letter to the editor of *Commentary* referred to *An American Family* as "essentially a woman-oriented series," providing some explanation for the correspondence Pat Loud received.[32] Apart from the facts that critics focused on Pat as the lead character in the show, that *An American Family* was positively reviewed in *Ms.* and *Vogue,* and that it was, mostly disparagingly, compared with soap operas, there were no other references to the documentary as a woman's picture. Interestingly, many of the reviewers of the program— including those most influential—were well-known feminists, such as Margaret Mead, Anne Roiphe, Abigail McCarthy, and Shana Alexander.[33]

Bill Loud, for his part, received a number of marriage proposals in the mail, as he mentioned on the Cavett show, including a letter from a woman in Georgia who stated, "If she doesn't want you, I do."[34] Lance, too, received a lot of correspondence: "I got three Bibles from different religious factions. Of course, they just burst into flames the second I opened the pages. And I got a lot of letters from gay guys—gay suburban kids—who thanked me for being a voice of outrage in a bland fucking normal middle-class world." In 1973, the year *An American Family* was broadcast, the American Psychiatric Association finally removed homosexuality from its list of mental disorders. Lance Loud did not come out on American TV; American television came out of the closet through *An American Family.* Writing in *Esquire* in November 1987, *New York Times* drama critic

Frank Rich singled out Lance's appearance as one of the defining images of a period he referred to as "the Gay Decade."[35]

Production secretary Alice Carey reflected in 1989 on Lance's pioneering role on TV: "*An American Family* wasn't so pro-gay in a political sense. Lance is hardly political as are a lot of gay men today. But in the series Lance was the embodiment of what it was like to be gay in that era, which was the adjective *gay*." As Anne Roiphe's review demonstrates, *An American Family* also provided occasions for homophobic responses as well as chances for viewers to identify with a gay character.[36] In an editorial in the *Chicago Tribune* titled "There Goes the Case for Gay Liberation," Jack Mabley complained that Lance's outrageous behavior gave homosexuality a bad name.[37] Today, however, the series is remembered with pride by the gay community and Lance is still occasionally recognized, and publicly thanked, on the streets of Los Angeles.

▶

Can a Documentary Be Made of Real Life?

On *The Dick Cavett Show*, Craig Gilbert admitted, with regret, that producers cannot control the reception of their works. *An American Family* amply illustrates this point. Although he believed the work would be controversial, Gilbert did not anticipate the harshness of the reviews, the hostility of the Louds, or the family's ensuing celebrity. The NET producer did

Lance Loud at the Chelsea Hotel in *An American Family*.

not expect critics to focus on the methods of observational filmmaking, nor did he imagine for a moment that his documentary would provide grist for attacks on the broadcast medium.[38]

The WNET publicity campaign set the agenda for responses to the program. Reviewers mostly read the series referentially, criticizing the Loud family. In *An American Family Revisited* (1983), Grant Loud pointed out, "Any jerk with a pencil or a typewriter, who had the audacity to write about us, sat in judgment of these people that he had never met." The program violated commonsense expectations, blurring genres across fiction and nonfiction. Mixing standards as the show mixed forms, critics compared *An American Family* primarily to dramatic programs. Many took the documentary as a moral tale about the decline of American culture. Others argued that intimate family life could not (and should not) be recorded on film, preferring the trusted conventions of television talk shows, investigative reports, and fiction. A vocal minority focused on the idea of the series; troubled by the premise of an observational cinema, many concluded that a documentary could not be made of real life.

Conclusion
The Children of *An American Family*

An American Family is not about us; it's about you. I don't want to tell you about what we're doing in our lives today.
:: Grant Loud[1]

▶

Long Live the Louds

In 1978, Susan Lester, the associate producer of *An American Family*, directed a thirty-minute television update about the Louds, *Five Years Later*, for ABC, the first in a ongoing stream of shows and articles that continues to this day. In 1993, *People* magazine profiled the family for the twentieth anniversary of the show.[2] Home Box Office (HBO) broadcast Susan and Alan Raymond's *An American Family Revisited: The Louds Ten Years Later* in 1983, a documentary that focuses on the media barrage following the broadcast of *An American Family*. Unlike the original series, it mixes interviews, archival photographs, and voice-over narration with scenes from the 1973 program. Once again, the Louds commanded the attention of the American media. Grant joked about their celebrity in the *Los Angeles Times*, "We even turn up in the crossword puzzles."[3]

An American Family Revisited was reviewed in the pages of *People*, *Time*, the *New York Times*, *TV Guide*, the *Los Angeles Times*, *Newsday*, *American Film*, the *Village Voice*, the *Christian Science Monitor*, *USA Today*, *Variety*, the *Chicago Tribune*, and many regional papers. Most critics saw *Revisited* as an opportunity to reflect on the supposed essential nature of TV, rather than an occasion to criticize the family as occurred in 1973. Admitting he was one of the "Loud freaks a decade ago," Peter Bunzel, in the *Los Angeles Herald Examiner*, argued that television is "a medium that thrives on reality," and Tom C. Smucker intoned, "Everyone wants to be validated—made real—by an appearance on TV," in the *Village Voice*.[4]

Many reviewers, reflecting back on the era (and paraphrasing the HBO press release) cited Linda Lovelace, the Watergate hearings, and the Louds as the main attractions of the 1973 season. Writing in *Time*, Richard Stengel surmised, "Television is proof positive of the theorem that the mere act of observing something changes the nature of the thing observed," and John Corry concluded in the *New York Times*, "The camera confirms existence."[5] Stephen Reddicliffe called attention to the ephemeral nature of the medium in the *Dallas Times Herald*, and Arthur Unger asked in the *Christian Science Monitor*, "Are we all becoming actors in a universal television soap opera?"[6]

These critics implied that the lessons learned from the original series had nothing to do with "the relations between men and women," "the generation gap," or "the American dream," as Gilbert's initial proposal anticipated, but rather reflected eternal verities about TV. Peggy Ziegler, the critic for *Multichannel News* in Denver, Colorado, underlined this fact: "*An American Family Revisited* ought to be seen by everybody who holds a pet theory about television and America."[7] At the end of *The Louds Ten Years Later*, Lance offers a last word on *An American Family*: "It was like a foreign film to me. It was great and strange, and you look back on it, and you think, 'That was life? That was really life? Or was what I remember of it life?'"

On December 31, 1990, in time for WNET's marathon rebroadcast of *An American Family* on New Year's Eve, the *New York Times* caught up with the Louds again. They found Lance living and working in Los Angeles as a freelance writer with a frequent byline in *American Film* and *Entertainment Weekly*. Kevin was in Houston, executive vice president of a business telephone company. His father, Bill, after retiring, had moved in with him. Grant made it to Hollywood, where he was acting in television commercials. Delilah, a marketing director for King World Television, was also living there. Michele was working in Manhattan at a children's clothing manufacturer, and Pat divided her time between a home in Bath, England, and Lance's Los Angeles apartment.

Susan and Alan Raymond now have a successful independent nonfiction production company, Video Verite. They have produced a string of social-issue documentaries for public, network, and cable television, including *The Police Tapes* (1977), an observational documentary about a precinct in the South Bronx that directly inspired the handheld shooting style of *Hill Street Blues* (1980–87). The Raymonds' prison documentary

Doing Time: Life inside the Big House (1991) was nominated for an Academy Award, and *I Am a Promise: The Children of Stanton Elementary School,* which chronicled a year in the lives of public school children in a poor Philadelphia neighborhood, won the Oscar for Best Feature Documentary in 1994.

In 1978, former NET president James Day accepted a teaching position at Brooklyn College. He retired in 1989 and published a personal history of public TV, *The Vanishing Vision: The Inside Story of Public Television,* which includes a chapter on *An American Family.*[8] Day remains critical of the current structure of public broadcasting. "*An American Family* could not have been done by PBS. My objection to PBS is simply that I don't think decision by committee is the way to make good programs. I think that, like partisan journalism, you have to have a hierarchical organization where there is an editor on top who sticks his or her neck out to take chances."

As a staff producer at NET, Gilbert did not have to worry about the distribution of his documentaries, nor did he own the programs on which he worked. Furthermore, he was always a writer and a producer who, like a Hollywood director, managed the technical performances of his crews. His background in TV led him to stylistic choices that never would have occurred to a Leacock or a Wiseman. Gilbert lost his staff position at WNET once *An American Family* was broadcast. Buffeted by criticisms of the series, he has not produced any other documentaries and his reputation has suffered over the years; textbooks such as Barnouw's *Documentary* ignore his contribution to the form. In 1988, he acknowledged, "I'm not considered a great documentary maker. Let's face up to it. I am still not accepted in the way that Wiseman is accepted, or Leacock, or Drew. I'm some kind of weird aberration out there on the fringe."

▶
_____

The Children of *An American Family*

Together with other innovative programs, *An American Family* recast the representation of family life on American television in the 1970s. Like *All in the Family* (1971–79), it explored the family as a site of conflict among couples and generations. Along with *The Mary Tyler Moore Show* (1970–77), the PBS documentary offered new definitions of gender roles and sexuality. In its aftermath, more diverse images of gays and lesbians gradually emerged on television in the mid-1970s.[9] In 1975, *One Day at a Time* became the first situation comedy to focus on a character who was a divorcée and single mother. Echoing Craig Gilbert, James L. Brooks, one of the producers of *The Mary Tyler Moore Show,* said, "The only issue I care about is that we don't recreate the old Ozzie and Harriet myth of an ideal family and an ideal world."[10] In the 1970s and 1980s, television talk shows greatly expanded the confessional and therapeutic impulses in American culture; their guests' intimate revelations went far beyond those of the Louds. Like *An American Family,* these shows emphasized family issues and interpersonal relationships. Eventually, hosts such as Oprah Winfrey joined in with personal disclosures of their own. In TV critic Michael Arlen's words, these talk shows took upon themselves "the demystification of the family."[11]

In his mock documentary *Real Life* (1979), film director Albert Brooks offered another kind of homage to *An American Family.*[12] *Real Life* opens with a crawl that promises to extend research undertaken in *An American Family:* "The motion picture you are about to see is the next step. It documents not only the life of a real family but of the real people who came to film that family and the effect they had on each other." With help from the "National Institute for Human Behavior," Brooks sets out to record the activities of a "typical American family," the Yeagers of Phoenix, Arizona, with many amusing consequences. *Real Life* ends with

Albert Brooks and the principal cast of his *Real Life.* Courtesy of Photofest.

a denunciation of the project by its social scientist consultant, the withdrawal of the family, and the burning of the Yeagers' home by a deranged Brooks, who hopes the fire will provide a dramatic climax for his movie. He rationalizes, "There's no law that says we can't start real and end fake. What are they going to do, put me in movie jail?"[13]

Although critics may read *An American Family* exclusively as the harbinger of the "society of the spectacle," its greater merit lies in opening up the institution of the family, and issues of gender, sexuality, and interpersonal relations, to serious nonfiction film and video.[14] Documentary filmmakers in the 1970s turned increasingly to intimate subject matter and first-person narration. Arguing that the personal is political, Joyce Chopra's *Joyce at 34* (1972), Amalie Rothschild's *Nana, Mom and Me* (1975), Miriam Weinstein's *We Get Married Twice* (1974), and Jill Godmilow's *Antonia: A Portrait of the Woman* (1974) explored issues in the growing women's movement. As Gilbert commenced work on his series, Ed Pincus embarked on his autobiographical epic *Diaries* (1982), adopting a loose chronological first-person narrative style, based on chance and the everyday, in which the filmmaker appears as the main character. Writing in *Filmmaker's Newsletter,* Pincus outlined his approach: "I have been shooting a film diary about my life and those around me since December 1971. I plan to continue the project for five years. For the first time I have been able to deal with the changes people undergo in their lives and consciousness over long periods of time."[15] *An American Family* accelerated and validated these new tendencies in nonfiction film style and subject matter.

For the coming generation of independent documentary filmmakers, Gilbert's series was a revelation. Beth Harrington, director of the autobiographical memoir *The Blinking Madonna and Other Miracles* (1996), discovered the power of nonfiction after seeing *An American Family* on television.[16] Mark Rance, who went on to study filmmaking at MIT with Ed Pincus and Richard Leacock, recalled watching *An American Family* "religiously," realizing in the process that "family life is the great subject of drama and the movies."[17] Rance took up one of the themes of *An American Family* in his stunning first-person debut, *Mom* (1978), which synthesized the observational style of Leacock with the participatory vision of Pincus. In *Mom*, Rance follows his middle-aged mother as she returns to school to explore a new career outside the home. At the end of the film, Mrs. Rance explodes at her cameraman/son, and this violent tirade, directed at the camera, places viewers in a difficult, compromised position. Rance's image of the family as a psychological battlefield is tempered somewhat in his feature-length portrait of his extended family, *Death and the Singing Telegram* (1982).

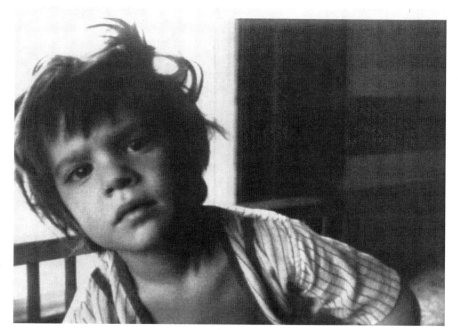

Ben Pincus in Ed Pincus's *Diaries*. Courtesy of Ed Pincus.

Beth Harrington, director of *The Blinking Madonna and Other Miracles*. Photograph by Catherine McDermott; courtesy of Beth Harrington.

Other filmmakers—many, like Rance, students of Pincus and Leacock at MIT in the 1970s—continued to push nonfiction into increasingly private terrain. In *Breaking and Entering* (1980), Ann Schaetzel returns home to even a score with her parents for destroying one of her teenage romantic relationships. Joel DeMott, daughter of literary critic Benjamin DeMott, produced a first-person documentary exposé, *Demon Lover Diary* (1979), of her boyfriend's work on a low-budget horror movie. In *Premature* (1981), David Parry focuses on the birth of his own premature child, blurring the boundaries of the educational film and personal documentary. In *Backyard* (1981), Ross McElwee returns to his parents' South Carolina home to film what he calls the "polite Carolina style of apartheid." His later *Sherman's March* (1986) ambles through the New South, combining conversations among family and friends with ruminations about sex, love, and war. *Time Indefinite* (1993) continues along these lines but explores McElwee's marriage, the death of his father, and the birth of his son.

Thanks to *An American Family*, interpersonal relations, family, gender, and sexuality have now become staples of American nonfiction film and video. Lise Yasui's *A Family Gathering* (1988) looks at her Japanese American family's experiences during World War II, the family's internment, and its aftermath. *Tongues Untied* (1991), Marlon Riggs's autobiographical tour de force of African American gay life, examines the inter-

Survivalists in Ross McElwee's *Sherman's March*. Courtesy of First Run Icarus Films and Ross McElwee.

The Yasui family album in Lise Yasui's *A Family Gathering*. Courtesy of the Yasui Family Archives and Lise Yasui.

section of race and sexuality in contemporary America. Jan Krawitz's *In Harm's Way* (1997) juxtaposes memories of growing up in Philadelphia with a violent rape that occurred at a Texas motel while the filmmaker was on location shooting her earlier documentary *Drive-In Blues* (1986).

First-person video diaries descend directly from terrain opened by Gilbert's documentary in the early 1970s. In *Trick or Drink* (1985), Vanalyne Green recalls a childhood dominated by her parents' alcoholism. As more and more intimate life comes under the gaze of independent videomakers, the revelations of *An American Family* pale by comparison. Peter Friedman and Tom Joslin's *Silverlake Life: The View from Here* (1993) chronicles the last months in a gay couple's twenty-two-year relationship as Joslin slowly succumbs to illnesses caused by AIDS. As these examples imply, *An American Family* represents a new stage in the filming of everyday lives of ordinary individuals, a landmark in the history of nonfiction film. In its aftermath, the American documentary would never be the same.

Notes

Preface

1. "Voyeur TV: We Like to Watch," *Time*, June 26, 2000.
2. Ronald Grover, "For CBS, *Survivor* Is a Strategy—and a Fountain of Youth," *Business Week Online*, June 20, 2000.
3. Theodore Roszak, *The Making of a Counterculture: Reflections on the Technological Society and Its Youthful Opposition* (New York: Doubleday, 1969).

Introduction

1. "The Divorce of the Year," *Newsweek*, March 12, 1973, 48.
2. Jay Sharbutt, "The Drama of TV's Last Real (?) Family," *Chicago Tribune*, February 27, 1973, 9. The quote from Donnet comes from an interview I conducted with her in 1989. All quotes in the text for which sources are not provided in notes come from my own interviews.
3. Merle Miller, "Dear Pat, Bill, Lance, Delilah, Grant, Kevin and Michele," *Esquire*, May, 1973, 239.
4. Quoted in Anne Roiphe, "*An American Family:* Things Are Keen but Could Be Keener," *New York Times Magazine*, February 18, 1973, 8.
5. Stephanie Harrington, "*An American Family* Lives Its Life on TV," *New York Times*, January 7, 1973, 5.
6. Pat Loud with Nora Johnson, *Pat Loud: A Woman's Story* (New York: Bantam, 1974), 8.
7. Margaret Mead, "As Significant as the Invention of Drama or the Novel," *TV Guide*, January 6, 1973, A61.
8. Shana Alexander, "The Silence of the Louds," *Newsweek*, January 22, 1973, 28; Shana Alexander, *The Feminine Eye* (New York: McCall, 1970).
9. Quoted in "The Broken Family: Divorce U.S. Style," *Newsweek*, March 12, 1973, 52.
10. Roiphe, "*An American Family*," 8, 41, 9.
11. Roger Rosenblatt, "Residuals on *An American Family*," *New Republic*, November 23, 1974, 21.
12. Michael Murray, "The Louds of Santa Barbara," *Commonweal*, March 23, 1973, 62.
13. Frank Rich, "The Gay Decade," *Esquire*, November 1987.
14. "And Another American Family," *Chicago Tribune*, March 3, 1973, 17.
15. Ella Taylor, *Prime-Time Families: Television Culture in Postwar America* (Berkeley: University of California Press, 1989).
16. Rick Altman, "Introduction," in *Sound Theory/Sound Practice*, ed. Rick Altman (New York: Routledge, Chapman, and Hall, 1992), 4.
17. Loud, *Pat Loud*, 123.
18. Robin Wood, "*Rules of the Game*," in *International Dictionary of Films and Filmmakers*, ed. Christopher Lyons (New York: Perigree Books, 1985), 390.
19. Quoted in Sybil Carlin, "Bye, Patty. Bye, Bill. Bye, Margaret," *Village Voice*, April 12, 1973, 25.
20. Mead, "As Significant as the Invention of Drama," A63.
21. In 1996, an earlier version of the manuscript for this book appeared in an installation by environmental sculptor Buster Simpson. Sponsored by the Santa Barbara Contemporary Arts Forum, Simpson's work was titled "The Silver Anniversary of *An American Family*" and was exhibited at 2615 Montrose Place in Santa Barbara. The manuscript, then titled *Family Programming*, appeared on a coffee table in the living room of the installation.

1. "A Real View of Middle-Class Life"

1. Craig Gilbert, "Reflections on *An American Family,*" *Studies in Visual Communication* 8, no. 1 (1982): 24.
2. Ibid., 50–54.
3. Les Brown, *Television: The Business behind the Box* (New York: Harcourt Brace Jovanovich, 1971), 198.
4. Robert J. Blakely, *To Serve the Public Interest: Educational Broadcasting in the United States* (Syracuse, N.Y.: Syracuse University Press, 1979), 134.
5. Erik Barnouw's *Documentary: A History of the Non-Fiction Film* (New York: Oxford University Press, 1974) has for years been the standard work in the field. Published in 1974, it makes no mention of *An American Family.* The revised edition of Barnouw's study that appeared in 1983 similarly ignores Gilbert's series.
6. Ved Mehta, *The Photographs of Chachaji: The Making of a Documentary Film* (New York: Oxford University Press, 1980), 227.
7. Gilbert, "Reflections on *An American Family,*" 25.
8. Quoted in Melinda Ward, "The Making of *An American Family,*" *Film Comment* 9 (November–December 1973): 30.
9. Gilbert, "Reflections on *An American Family,*" 26.
10. Quoted in Alan Rosenthal, *The New Documentary in Action: A Casebook in Film Making* (Berkeley: University of California Press, 1971), 23.
11. Gilbert, "Reflections on *An American Family,*" 26.
12. Pat Loud with Nora Johnson, *Pat Loud: A Woman's Story* (New York: Bantam, 1974), 80.
13. Theodore Roszak, *The Making of a Counterculture: Reflections on the Technological Society and Its Youthful Opposition* (New York: Doubleday, 1969); Charles A. Reich, *The Greening of America* (New York: Bantam, 1970).
14. Keith Melville, *Marriage and Family Today* (New York: Random House, 1977), 240.
15. Reich, *The Greening of America,* 79.
16. Horace Newcomb and Robert S. Alley, *The Producer's Medium: Conversations with Creators of American TV* (New York: Oxford University Press, 1983), 200.
17. Alan Raymond and Susan Raymond, "Filming *An American Family,*" *Filmmaker's Newsletter,* March 6, 1973, 19.
18. Melville, *Marriage and Family Today,* 377.
19. Gilbert, "Reflections on *An American Family,*" 27.
20. James Day, *The Vanishing Vision: The Inside Story of Public Television* (Berkeley: University of California Press, 1995), 186.
21. Brown, *Television,* 324.
22. Paul Wilkes, *Six American Families* (New York: Parthenon, 1977), 133.
23. Quoted in Barbara Zheutlin, "The Politics of Documentary: A Symposium," in *New Challenges for Documentary,* ed. Alan Rosenthal (Berkeley: University of California Press, 1988), 237.
24. Gilbert, "Reflections on *An American Family,*" 27.
25. Melville, *Marriage and Family Today,* 387.
26. Cecil Smith, "Finding—and Filming—an American Family," *Los Angeles Times,* January 11, 1973, 22.
27. Bernard Schopen, *Ross Macdonald* (Boston: Twayne, 1990), 17.
28. Robert Kirsch, "Ross Macdonald: *The Underground Man,*" *Los Angeles Times,* March 14, 1971, 62.
29. Reich, *The Greening of America,* 274.
30. Loud, *Pat Loud,* 80.
31. Using the overall Consumer Price Index, with inflation increasing approximately 352 percent from 1973 through 1998, Craig Gilbert's salary in 1998 dollars would be around $3,390 per week: $750/week x 4.52 (1 + 3.52). By way of comparison, the minimum wage in 1970 was $1.60/hour, or $64 a week.
32. Craig Gilbert and Susan Lester, "The Proposal," unpublished WNET document, 1971, 1.
33. Gilbert, "Reflections on *An American Family,*" 30–40.
34. Gilbert and Lester, "The Proposal," 1.
35. Loud, *Pat Loud,* 64.
36. Gilbert and Lester, "The Proposal," 19–20.
37. Ibid., 12, 14, 2.
38. Gilbert, "Reflections on *An American Family,*" 54.
39. Gilbert and Lester, "The Proposal," 21.
40. Tamar Liebes and Elihu Katz, *The Export of Meaning: Cross Cultural Readings of "Dallas"* (New York: Oxford University Press, 1990), 123.

41. Anne Roiphe, "An American Family: Things Are Keen but Could Be Keener," New York Times Magazine, February 18, 1973, 45.
42. Quoted in "Sample of One?" Time, February 26, 1973, 51.

2. Filming the Louds, Editing the Footage

1. Using the overall Consumer Price Index, with inflation increasing approximately 352 percent from 1973 through 1998, Alan Raymond's salary in 1998 dollars would be about $4,520 per week: $1,000/week x 4.52 (1 + 3.52).
2. Craig Gilbert, "An American Family—the Credit Confusion," New York Times, October 18, 1994, A19.
3. Pat Loud with Nora Johnson, Pat Loud: A Woman's Story (New York: Bantam, 1974), 105–6.
4. Craig Gilbert, "Reflections on An American Family," Studies in Visual Communication 8, no. 1 (1982): 34.
5. Ibid., 30.
6. Thomas R. Atkins, Frederick Wiseman (New York: Monarch, 1976), 72.
7. Jay Ruby, "Speaking for, Speaking about, Speaking with, or Speaking Alongside: An Anthropological and Documentary Dilemma," Journal of Film and Video 44, nos. 1–2 (1992): 42–66.
8. Gilbert, "Reflections on An American Family," 30, 31.
9. Ved Mehta, The Photographs of Chachaji: The Making of a Documentary Film (New York: Oxford University Press, 1980).
10. Roger Silverstone, Framing Science: The Making of a BBC Documentary (London: British Film Institute, 1985), 129.
11. Before her cameo in An American Family, Curtis performed in Andy Warhol and Paul Morrissey's Flesh (1968) and Women in Revolt (1972) as well as in Dusan Makavejev's WR: Mysteries of the Organism (1971).
12. Loud, Pat Loud, 87.
13. "An American Family," Newsweek, January 15, 1973, 68.
14. Loud, Pat Loud, 88.
15. Quoted in Melinda Ward, "The Making of An American Family," Film Comment 9 (November–December, 1973), 31.
16. Loud, Pat Loud, 104.
17. Ibid., 95.
18. Gilbert, "Reflections on An American Family," 34.
19. Alan Raymond and Susan Raymond, "An American Family," American Cinematographer, May 1973, 605, 592.
20. Ibid., 594.
21. The Reminiscences of Alan and Susan Raymond (New York: Oral History Collection of Columbia University, 1980), 25.
22. Raymond and Raymond, "An American Family," 605.
23. Ibid., 592, 593. A Lowell Softlight brightened the living room, and the crew mounted Lowell D quartz lights to the walls of some of the other rooms. For actions filmed outdoors at night, Alan occasionally used a hundred-watt sun gun lamp attached to the camera. Indoors, Raymond used Eastman tungsten-balanced 7242 reversal stock, and for outdoor scenes, he used the daylight-balanced ECT 7252 reversal. When necessary, the footage was push-processed one to two f-stops at CFI labs in Hollywood, allowing Alan to shoot at f-3.2 inside the house, an f-stop that retained some depth of field.
24. Ibid., 604.
25. Quoted in David Edelstein, "A Date with History," Village Voice, September 9, 1985.
26. Alan Raymond and Susan Raymond, "Filming An American Family," Filmmaker's Newsletter, March 6, 1973, 20.
27. Loud, Pat Loud, 99.
28. Quoted in "Real-Life Louds Recall Their Days as TV's Louds," Chicago Tribune, April 22, 1973, 2.
29. Quoted in Ward, "The Making of An American Family," 26.
30. Loud, Pat Loud, 113.
31. Ibid., 116–17.
32. Ibid., 119–20.
33. Joan Churchill has had a successful career as a cinematographer on independent documentaries and features. Her credits include Punishment Park (1971), Lily Tomlin (1986), and Kurt & Courtney (1998). She also codirected Soldier Girls (1981) with then-husband Nick Broomfield.
34. John Terry, "An American Family in Super-8," Filmmaker's Newsletter, March 6, 1973, 22–23. With this prototype of extremely lightweight film technology, sound recordist Mecklinberg employed an

AKG-D-190E dynamic cardiod microphone. Cinematographer John Terry used Kodak SO-105 Super-8mm film stock—the equivalent of the outdoor stock Raymond used—at 125 ASA, although it was frequently push-processed. Smaller and less obtrusive than the 16mm equipment used by the others, the Super-8 format represented significant savings over 16mm. John Terry is currently the head of the Department of Film/Animation/Video at the Rhode Island School of Design.

35. Loud, *Pat Loud*, 122.
36. Ibid., 123.
37. Ibid., 127.
38. Zwerin also edited the Maysles brothers' *With Love from Truman: A Visit with Truman Capote* (1966) and *Salesman* (1969). More recently she has directed independent documentaries of her own, *Thelonious Monk: Straight, No Chaser* (1989) and *Music for the Movies: Toru Takemitsu* (1994).
39. Gilbert, "Reflections on *An American Family*," 39.
40. Ibid., 37.
41. Patricia Jaffe, "Editing Cinéma Vérité," *Film Comment* 3 (summer 1965): 43–47.
42. Quoted in Gabriella Oldham, *First Cut: Conversations with Film Editors* (Berkeley: University of California Press, 1992), 45.
43. Quoted in ibid., 117.
44. Gilbert, "Reflections on *An American Family*," 53.
45. While he was vice president for programming, Robert Kotlowitz was a strong supporter of Frederick Wiseman's work, which received significant backing from WNET. Kotlowitz has since published a series of novels, *The Boardwalk* (New York: Alfred A. Knopf, 1976), *Sea Changes* (New York: North Point, 1986), and *His Master's Voice* (New York: Alfred A. Knopf, 1992). Like many of the professional critics of *An American Family*, Kotlowitz has made his own personal experiences public in a memoir, *Before Their Time* (New York: Random House, 1997).
46. Gilbert, "Reflections on *An American Family*," 37–38.
47. This citation echoes the use, in episode one, of "Boogie Woogie Bugle Boy," an Andrews Sisters song made famous by the earlier *Buck Privates* (1941).
48. Gilbert, "Reflections on *An American Family*," 48.
49. A. William Bluem, *Documentary in American Television: Form, Function, Method* (New York: Hastings House, 1965), 131.
50. Loud, *Pat Loud*, 125.
51. Quoted in "Real-Life Louds," 2.
52. Loud, *Pat Loud*, 124.
53. Elinor Bunin also created the title sequence for Robert Rossen's feature film *Lilith* (1964) and later did the same for the PBS documentary series *Six American Families* (1976).
54. Loud, *Pat Loud*, 133.

3. "A Bastard Union of Several Forms"

1. P. J. O'Connell, *Robert Drew and the Development of Cinema Verite in America* (Carbondale: Southern Illinois University Press, 1992), 34.
2. Stephen Mamber, *Cinema Verite in America: Studies in Uncontrolled Documentary* (Cambridge: MIT Press, 1974), 115–38.
3. Jean-Claude Bringuier, "Libres propos sur le cinéma-vérité," *Cahiers du Cinéma* 25 (July 1963): 16.
4. David MacDougall, "Observational Cinema," in *Principles of Visual Anthropology*, ed. Paul Hockings (The Hague: Mouton, 1975), 112.
5. Quoted in James Hindman and Victoria Costello, eds., *The Independent Documentary: The Implications of Diversity, a Conference Report* (Washington, D.C.: American Film Institute, 1983), 47.
6. Quoted in G. Roy Levin, *Documentary Explorations: 15 Interviews with Film-Makers* (New York: Doubleday, 1971), 238–39.
7. Quoted in O'Connell, *Robert Drew*, 32.
8. Quoted in Levin, *Documentary Explorations*, 227.
9. Unlike Gilbert, Frederick Wiseman was a lawyer more fascinated with European art film, American independent cinema, and the contemporary novel than with television. Wiseman learned how to make films by producing Shirley Clarke's independent fiction film *The Cool World* (1963) and by collaborating with ethnographic filmmaker John Marshall on *Titicut Follies* in 1967. Wiseman's ties to WNET-13 eventually became very strong, but he retained artistic and financial control over all his films, working as sound recordist, editor, director, producer, and distributor.
10. John Ellis, *Visible Fictions: Cinema, Television, Video* (London: Routledge & Kegan Paul, 1982), 150.
11. Robert C. Allen, *Speaking of Soap Operas* (Chapel Hill: University of North Carolina Press, 1985).

12. Tamar Liebes and Elihu Katz, *The Export of Meaning: Cross Cultural Readings of "Dallas"* (New York: Oxford University Press, 1990), 10.
13. Roger Rosenblatt, "Residuals on *An American Family*," *New Republic*, November 23, 1974, 21.

4. Opening Night

1. John Ellis, *Visible Fictions: Cinema, Television, Video* (London: Routledge & Kegan Paul, 1982), 119–20.
2. Jay Leyda, *Films Beget Films* (New York: Hill & Wang, 1964), 24.
3. Ellis, *Visible Fictions*, 150.

5. Sound in Documentary

1. Rick Altman, "The Technology of the Voice I," *Iris* 3, no. 1 (1985): 3–20; Rick Altman, "The Technology of the Voice II," *Iris* 4, no. 1 (1986): 107–18.
2. Noël Carroll, *Mystifying Movies: Fads and Fallacies of Contemporary Film Theory* (New York: Columbia University Press, 1988), 180.
3. David Bordwell, Janet Staiger, and Kristin Thompson, *The Classical Hollywood Cinema: Film Style and Mode of Production to 1960* (New York: Columbia University Press, 1985), 93.
4. Rick Altman, "Sound Space," in *Sound Theory/Sound Practice*, ed. Rick Altman (New York: Routledge, Chapman, & Hall, 1992), 61–62.
5. Sarah Kozloff, *Invisible Storytellers: Voice-Over Narration in American Fiction Film* (Berkeley: University of California Press, 1988), 21.
6. Thomas Benson and Carolyn Anderson, "The Rhetorical Structure of Frederick Wiseman's *Model*," *Journal of Film and Video* 36, no. 4 (1984): 31.
7. Dell Hymes, "Models of the Interaction of Language and Social Life," in *Directions in Sociolinguistics*, ed. John J. Gumperz and Dell Hymes (New York: Holt, Rinehart & Winston, 1972), 40.
8. Michel Marie, "Direct," in *Anthropology-Reality-Cinema: The Films of Jean Rouch*, ed. Mick Eaton (London: British Film Institute, 1979), 39.
9. Michael Rabiger, *Directing the Documentary* (Boston: Focal Press, 1987), 59–60.
10. Quoted in Mark Singer, "Predilections," *New Yorker*, February 6, 1989, 48.
11. Roger Silverstone, *Framing Science: The Making of a BBC Documentary* (London: British Film Institute, 1985), 69.
12. Bill Nichols, "The Voice of Documentary," *Film Quarterly* 36, no. 3 (1983): 17–30.
13. Quoted in Irv Broughton, ed., *Producers on Producing: The Making of Film and Television* (Jefferson, N.C.: McFarland, 1986), 126.
14. Stephen Mamber, *Cinema Verite in America: Studies in Uncontrolled Documentary* (Cambridge: MIT Press, 1974), 4.
15. Independent producer Tony Buba addresses this issue in an amusing scene in *Lightning over Braddock* (1989), in which a song by the Rolling Stones is pointedly *not* heard on the sound track. As we watch a mock performance of the tune by local teenagers in a bar in Braddock, Pennsylvania, Buba muses in voice-over that the rights to the song, which played on the jukebox, would have cost $10,000. He adds that if he had paid such an extravagant amount of money, given the subject of his low-budget film, which is about economic downturn in the rust belt during the Reagan years, St. Peter would not allow him into heaven.
16. See Claudia Gorbman, *Unheard Melodies: Narrative Film Music* (Bloomington: Indiana University Press, 1987).
17. For the most part, Wiseman avoids such editorial uses of music in his later films. The absence of music in *Hospital* contributes to its oppressive atmosphere of suffering and pain. A young man who overdoses on mescaline begs his attendants to "play some music or sing" to relieve his anxiety.
18. After the documentary was broadcast, in a turn of events in which life may be seen imitating art, the Loud children performed several tunes as a group on *The Dick Cavett Show* and other TV programs. Meanwhile, Lance capitalized on his newfound celebrity by forming the Mumps, a punk rock group that played original music in New York City clubs throughout the 1970s. In the Raymonds' remake, *An American Family Revisited: The Louds Ten Years Later* (1983), Grant pursues a career as a lounge singer in Southern California nightspots.
19. Anne Roiphe, "*An American Family*: Things Are Keen but Could Be Keener," *New York Times Magazine*, February 18, 1973, 53.
20. E. Ann Kaplan, "Theories and Strategies of Feminist Documentary," in *New Challenges for Documentary*, ed. Alan Rosenthal (Berkeley: University of California Press, 1988), 80.
21. Richard Dyer, *Heavenly Bodies: Film Stars and Society* (New York: St. Martin's, 1986), 178.
22. S. I. Hayakawa, "Can a Documentary Be Made of Real Life?" *Chicago Tribune*, March 11, 1973, 6.

6. Publicity Sets the Stage, Reviews Steal the Show

1. Jay Ruby, "The Image Mirrored: Reflexivity and the Documentary Film," *Journal of the University Film Association* 29, no. 4 (1977): 3–13; Jay Ruby, "Exposing Yourself: Reflexivity, Film, and Anthropology," *Semiotica* 30, nos. 1–2 (1980): 153–79; Jay Ruby, "Ethnography as Trompe L'Oeil: Film and Anthropology," in *A Crack in the Mirror: Reflexive Perspectives in Anthropology,* ed. Jay Ruby (Philadelphia: University of Pennsylvania Press, 1982), 121–32.
2. Bill Nichols, *Representing Reality: Issues and Concepts in Documentary* (Bloomington: Indiana University Press, 1991), 18.
3. Quoted in Pat Loud with Nora Johnson, *Pat Loud: A Woman's Story* (New York: Bantam, 1974), 142.
4. Janet Staiger, *Interpreting Films: Studies in the Historical Reception of American Cinema* (Princeton, N.J.: Princeton University Press, 1992).
5. WNET, "Background Production Information," in *An American Family* press packet, 1973, 1.
6. Ibid., 2.
7. See Rupert Wilkinson, *The Pursuit of American Character* (New York: Harper & Row, 1988), 30.
8. WNET, "Profile of the William C. Loud Family," in *An American Family* press packet, 1973, 1.
9. WNET, "Press Release," in *An American Family* press packet, 1973, 3.
10. "An American Family," *TV Guide*, January 6, 1973, A61.
11. WNET, "Press Release," 3.
12. John J. O'Connor, "TV: *An American Family* Is a Provocative Series," *New York Times*, January 23, 1973, 1.
13. Merle Miller, "Dear Pat, Bill, Lance, Delilah, Grant, Kevin and Michele," *Esquire*, May 1973, 240.
14. Anne Roiphe, "*An American Family*: Things Are Keen but Could Be Keener," *New York Times Magazine*, February 18, 1973, 46.
15. Miller, "Dear Pat, Bill, Lance," 240. See also Merle Miller, *On Being Different: What It Means to Be a Homosexual* (New York: Popular Library, 1971).
16. Loud, *Pat Loud*, 142.
17. Craig Gilbert, "Reflections on *An American Family*," *Studies in Visual Communication* 8, no. 1 (1982): 53.
18. Quoted in Michael Murray, "The Louds of Santa Barbara," *Commonweal*, March 23, 1973, 60.
19. John J. O'Connor, "TV: Arguments over *An American Family* Are Smothering Its Contents," *New York Times*, January 22, 1973, 3.
20. Stephanie Harrington, "*An American Family* Lives Its Life on TV," *New York Times*, January 7, 1973, 5.
21. Gail Rock, "All in a Real Family," *Ms.*, February 1973, 22.
22. Roger Rosenblatt, "Residuals on *An American Family*," *New Republic*, November 23, 1974, 20. Like so many other professional critics of *An American Family*, Rosenblatt recently wrote a confessional memoir of his own, *Coming Apart: A Memoir of the Harvard Wars of 1969* (Boston: Little, Brown, 1997).
23. Murray, "The Louds of Santa Barbara," 60; Harrington, "*An American Family*," 19.
24. Tamar Liebes and Elihu Katz, *The Export of Meaning: Cross Cultural Readings of "Dallas"* (New York: Oxford University Press, 1990), 100.
25. Shana Alexander, "The Silence of the Louds," *Newsweek*, January 22, 1973, 28.
26. Roiphe, "*An American Family*," 46.
27. Ibid., 45.
28. Sol Worth, *Studying Visual Communication*, ed. Larry Gross (Philadelphia: University of Pennsylvania Press, 1981), 173.
29. Roiphe, "*An American Family*," 8.
30. Bruce Voeller, "Letter to the Editor," *New York Times Magazine*, March 4, 1973, 4.
31. Vito Russo, *The Celluloid Closet: Homosexuality in the Movies*, rev. ed. (New York: Harper & Row, 1987), 220.
32. Roiphe, "*An American Family*," 53; Anne Roiphe, "Ma and Pa and John Boy in Mythic America: The Waltons," *New York Times Magazine*, November 18, 1973, 40 ff.
33. "The Divorce of the Year," *Newsweek*, March 12, 1973, 48.
34. John Ellis, *Visible Fictions: Cinema, Television, Video* (London: Routledge & Kegan Paul, 1982), 132.
35. "Sample of One?" *Time*, February 26, 1973, 52.
36. Stanley Kauffmann, "Filming Filming," *New Republic*, April 1979, 24.
37. In a prescient discussion at the end of *Chronicle of a Summer* (Jean Rouch and Edgar Morin, 1961), sociologist Edgar Morin sums up this reaction to documentaries about intimate life: "As soon as people are a little more sincere than they are in real life, others say either 'You're a ham, an actor,' or else they say, 'You're an exhibitionist.'" Translated in "*Chronicle of a Summer*—the Film," *Studies in Visual Communication* 11, no. 1 (1985): 69.
38. Sara Sanborn, "*An American Family*," *Commentary*, May 1973, 80.

39. Bruce E. Gronbeck, "The Academic Practice of Television Criticism," *Quarterly Journal of Speech* 74 (1988): 334–35.

40. Crawford Woods, "The Louds," *New Republic*, March 24, 1973, 23.

41. Murray, "The Louds of Santa Barbara," 62. One year later, Murray published *The Videotape Book: A Basic Guide to Portable TV Production for Families, Friends, Schools and Neighborhoods* (New York: Bantam, 1974). A blurb on the book's cover claims there is "no need to settle for regularly scheduled network programming once you've discovered how simple, inexpensive and exciting it is to put yourself on TV." For other reviewers, the only possible response was parody. In the *Chicago Tribune*, one critic proposed a new series about the Scrimshaws of Florida: "We'll start filming the family just as soon as Everett Jr. gives my documentary crew its camera back and apologizes for throttling the producer." Jay Sharbutt, "The Drama of TV's Last Real (?) Family," *Chicago Tribune*, February 27, 1973, 9.

42. Stephanie Harrington, "Of Loneliness and Publicity," *The Nation*, September 14, 1974, 220.

43. Pat Loud, "Some Second Thoughts from *An American Family*," *Los Angeles Times*, March 4, 1973, 7.

44. Quoted in Jon Nordheimer, "He Feels Like a Kid Again, but His *American Family* Is in Ruins," *New York Times*, March 1, 1974, 1.

45. Margaret Mead, *Blackberry Winter: My Earlier Years* (New York: William Morrow, 1972); Shana Alexander, *State-by-State Guide to Women's Legal Rights* (Los Angeles: Wollstonecraft, 1975); Anne Roiphe, *Up the Sandbox!* (New York: Simon and Schuster, 1970); Abigail McCarthy, *Private Faces/Public Places* (New York: Doubleday, 1972). In 1972, Irvin Kershner directed a feature film version of *Up the Sandbox* that starred Barbra Streisand.

46. "Spy Drama," *The Nation*, March 5, 1973, 293.

47. S. I. Hayakawa, "Can a Documentary Be Made of Real Life?" *Chicago Tribune*, March 11, 1973, 6; "Spy Drama," 293.

48. Noël Carroll, "From Real to Reel: Entangled in Nonfiction Film," *Philosophic Exchange* 14 (1983): 24.

49. Robert C. Allen, *Speaking of Soap Operas* (Chapel Hill: University of North Carolina Press, 1985), 91.

50. Sharbutt, "The Drama of TV's Last Real (?) Family," 9; "The Divorce of the Year," 49; Hayakawa, "Can a Documentary Be Made of Real Life?" 6.

51. Alexander, "The Silence of the Louds," 28; Sanborn, "*An American Family*," 79; John J. O'Connor, "Mr. & Mrs. Loud, Meet the Bradys," *New York Times*, March 4, 1973, 19.

52. Erica Brown, "*An American Family*: Alive on the Screen," *Vogue*, January 1973, 68.

53. WNET, "Episodes," in *An American Family* press packet, 1973, 1.

54. See, for example, "The Broken Family: Divorce U.S. Style," *Newsweek*, March 12, 1973, 47–48, 50, 55, 57.

55. "Sample of One?" 51–52.

56. WNET, "Press Release," 2.

57. O'Connor, "Mr. & Mrs. Loud," 19; Miller, "Dear Pat, Bill, Lance," 242; Dan Menaker "*An American Family*," *Harper's*, March 1973, 99.

58. "*An American Family*," *Chicago Tribune*, January 11, 1973, 9.

59. Miller's comment appears on the cover of Howard Junker, ed., *Salesman* (New York: Signet, 1969).

60. Robert Geller, "Coming of Age in Santa Barbara: *An American Family*," *Media and Methods*, March 9, 1973, 50.

61. Harrington, "*An American Family*," 5.

62. O'Connor, "TV: *An American Family*," 79.

63. Harrington, "*An American Family*" 5.

64. Liebes and Katz, *The Export of Meaning*, 100.

65. Jim Gaines, "TV: The Decline and Fall of an American Family," *Saturday Review of the Arts*, January 1973, 47.

66. Ibid., 48.

67. "The Divorce of the Year," 49.

68. David Bordwell, Janet Staiger, and Kristin Thompson, *The Classical Hollywood Cinema: Film Style and Mode of Production to 1960* (New York: Columbia University Press, 1985), 19.

69. Loud, *Pat Loud*, 115.

70. Quoted in Clarence Petersen, "'We Were Very Naive about a Lot,'" *Chicago Tribune*, March 22, 1973, 6.

71. Bill Nichols, "The Voice of Documentary," *Film Quarterly* 36, no. 3 (1983): 17–30.

72. Colin Young, "The Family," *Sight and Sound* 43, no. 4 (1974): 207.

73. "Sample of One?" 51; Rock, "All in a Real Family," 22; Alexander, "The Silence of the Louds," 23.

74. O'Connor, "Mr. & Mrs. Loud, " 19.

75. Alexander, "The Silence of the Louds," 28.

76. "An American Family," *TV Guide*, February 3, 1973, A58.
77. "An American Family," *Newsweek*, January 15, 1973, 68; Rock, "All in a Real Family," 22; "An American Family," *America*, February 10, 1973, 111.
78. O'Connor, "TV: An American Family," 1; Woods, "The Louds," 23; Alexander, "The Silence of the Louds," 28; John W. Donohue, "Afterthoughts on *An American Family*," *America*, April 28, 1973, 390; Menaker, "An American Family," 98.
79. Quoted in Roiphe, "An American Family," 51.
80. Abigail McCarthy, "An American Family and The Family of Man," *Atlantic*, July 1973, 73.
81. Nancy Aruffo, "Letter to the Editor," *New York Times*, March 11, 1973, 99.
82. Quoted in "An American Family," *Newsweek*, 68.
83. Robert Geller, "Coming of Age in Santa Barbara," 50.
84. Arlene Skolnick, *Embattled Paradise: The American Family in an Age of Uncertainty* (New York: Basic Books, 1991), 128.
85. Wilkinson, *The Pursuit of American Character*, 72.
86. Charles A. Reich, *The Greening of America* (New York: Bantam, 1970), 22.
87. Quoted in "The Divorce of the Year," 49.
88. Quoted in ibid.
89. Geller, "Coming of Age in Santa Barbara" 50.
90. Murray, "The Louds of Santa Barbara," 62.
91. Roiphe, "An American Family," 53.
92. Quoted in Donohue, "Afterthoughts on *An American Family*," 390.
93. Gilbert, "Reflections on *An American Family*," 47–48.
94. Donohue, "Afterthoughts on *An American Family*," 390.
95. Quoted in ibid.
96. "Sample of One?" 51.
97. "Spy Drama," 293.
98. "Sample of One?" 52.
99. "The Divorce of the Year," 49.
100. Quoted in Sybil Carlin, "Bye, Patty. Bye, Bill. Bye, Margaret," *Village Voice*, April 12, 1973, 25.
101. Hayakawa, "Can a Documentary Be Made of Real Life?" 6.
102. Carol Kramer, "Looking thru the Lens at One Man's Family," *Chicago Tribune*, February 1, 1973, 1–2.
103. O'Connor, "TV: Arguments over *An American Family*," 7.
104. Quoted in "The Divorce of the Year," 48.
105. Quoted in Cecil Smith, "Finding—and Filming—an American Family," *Los Angeles Times*, January 11, 1973, 22.
106. Sanborn, "An American Family"; McCarthy, "An American Family and The Family of Man"; Murray, "The Louds of Santa Barbara."
107. Gilbert, "Reflections on *An American Family*," 53.
108. Ibid., 44.
109. Murray, "The Louds of Santa Barbara," 62.
110. Melinda Ward, "The Making of *An American Family*," *Film Comment* 9 (November–December 1973): 27.
111. Gilbert, "Reflections on *An American Family*," 34.
112. "An American Family," *America*, 111.
113. Hayakawa, "Can a Documentary Be Made of Real Life?" 6.
114. Menaker, "An American Family," 98.
115. "Spy Drama," 293; Woods, "The Louds," 23.
116. Sanborn, "An American Family," 80.
117. Hayakawa, "Can a Documentary Be Made of Real Life?" 6.
118. Gilbert, "Reflections on *An American Family*," 49.
119. "Sample of One?" 52.
120. "The Divorce of the Year," 49.
121. Woods, "The Louds," 23; Donohue, "Afterthoughts on *An American Family*," 390; Hayakawa, "Can a Documentary Be Made of Real Life?" 6; Sanborn, "An American Family," 78.
122. Dai Vaughan, "The Aesthetics of Ambiguity," in *Film as Ethnography*, ed. Peter Ian Crawford and David Turton (Manchester: Manchester University Press, 1992), 100.

7. The Louds Strike Back

1. Quoted in "Sample of One?" *Time*, February 26, 1973.
2. Pat Loud with Nora Johnson, *Pat Loud: A Woman's Story* (New York: Bantam, 1974), 124.

3. Quoted in Craig Gilbert, "Reflections on *An American Family*," *Studies in Visual Communication* 8, no. 1 (1982): 41.

4. *"An American Family,"* *Newsweek*, January 15, 1973, 68.

5. John Ellis, *Visible Fictions: Cinema, Television, Video* (London: Routledge & Kegan Paul, 1982), 91.

6. Dwight Hoover, *Middletown: The Making of a Documentary Film Series* (Philadelphia: Harwood, 1992), 111. *Seventeen* was one of six films in the public television series *Middletown*, which was independently produced by documentary filmmaker Peter Davis.

7. Quoted in "Ultimate Soap Opera," *Time*, January 22, 1973, 36.

8. Sybil Carlin, "Seeing the Loud Family," *Village Voice*, March 1, 1973, 15.

9. "Real-Life Louds Recall Their Days as TV's Louds," *Chicago Tribune*, April 22, 1973, 2.

10. Jeanne Lynn Hall, "Refracting Reality: The Early Films of Robert Drew and Associates" (Ph.D. diss., University of Wisconsin–Madison, Department of Communication Arts, 1990), 21.

11. Clarence Petersen, "Loud Family May Be Broken—but It's Not Broke," *Chicago Tribune*, March 21, 1973, 1.

12. Stephanie Harrington, "Of Loneliness and Publicity," *The Nation*, September 14, 1974, 220.

13. Quoted in Petersen, "Loud Family May Be Broken," 6.

14. Quoted in "Sample of One?" 51.

15. Loud, *Pat Loud*, 11. Despite the upheaval caused by the broadcast of *An American Family*, the Louds were still eager to support their local public television station, KCET.

16. Michael Murray, "The Louds of Santa Barbara," *Commonweal*, March 23, 1973, 60.

17. Ron Goulart, ed., *An American Family* (New York: Warner Paperback Library, 1973).

18. Nora Johnson is the daughter of Hollywood producer, director, and screenwriter Nunnally Johnson, who directed *The Man Who Understood Women* (1959) and wrote the screenplay for *The Dirty Dozen* (1967), among many other works. Working with her father, she turned her own story, *The World of Henry Orient*, into a screenplay that was filmed by George Roy Hill in 1964. Nora Johnson has since published many novels, a book about her father, and a memoir, *You Can Go Home Again: An Intimate Journey* (New York: Doubleday, 1982).

19. Quoted in Gregg Kilday, "The Rerun Life of Pat Loud," *Los Angeles Times*, May 2, 1974, 14.

20. Robert Kirsch, "Pat Loud: A Part of the Age of Exposure," *Los Angeles Times*, April 28, 1974, 62.

21. Loud, *Pat Loud*, 83–84.

22. Ibid., 60–79.

23. Anne Roiphe, "*An American Family*: Things Are Keen but Could Be Keener," *New York Times Magazine*, February 18, 1973, 52.

24. Quoted in Stephen Mamber, *Cinema Verite in America: Studies in Uncontrolled Documentary* (Cambridge: MIT Press, 1974), 240–41.

25. Harry F. Waters, "Wiseman's *Near Death*," *Newsweek*, January 22, 1990, 52.

26. WNET, "The Family," in *An American Family* press packet, 1973, 1.

27. Abigail McCarthy, "*An American Family* and *The Family of Man*," *Atlantic*, July 1973, 74.

28. Loud, *Pat Loud*, 8.

29. Ibid., 158.

30. Ibid., 156–58.

31. Gail Rock, "All in a Real Family," *Ms.*, February 1973, 23.

32. F. M. Conn, "Letter to the Editor," *Commentary*, October 1973, 16.

33. Shana Alexander later penned a tell-all memoir, *Happy Days: My Mother, My Father, My Sister and Me* (New York: Doubleday, 1995). In addition to profiling her family life—Cecelia Ager, her mother, was a movie critic for *Variety*, among other publications, and her father, Milton, composed popular songs—Alexander describes her own successful career as a cultural commentator at *Life*, *McCall's*, and *Newsweek*, and on the television newsmagazine *60 Minutes*.

34. Quoted in Loud, *Pat Loud*, 155.

35. Frank Rich, "The Gay Decade," *Esquire*, November 1987.

36. In the intervening years, Anne Roiphe has produced a string of first-person books of cultural commentary, including *Generation without Memory: A Jewish Journey in Christian America* (Boston: Beacon, 1981), *Fruitful: A Real Mother in the Modern World* (New York: Penguin, 1996), and an autobiography, *1185 Park Avenue: A Memoir* (New York: Free Press, 1999), which recounts her childhood growing up on the Upper East Side in Manhattan. She still owes Lance Loud an apology for her 1973 review of *An American Family*.

37. Jack Mabley, "There Goes the Case for Gay Liberation," *Chicago Tribune*, March 25, 1973, 4.

38. Gilbert, "Reflections on *An American Family*," 45–6.

Conclusion

1. Grant Loud made this statement during a public discussion of *An American Family* at the Museum of Broadcasting in 1988.

2. Craig Horowitz, "Reality Check," *People*, March 22, 1993, 61–63.
3. Quoted in David Crook, "The Louds Revisited—on Pay TV," *Los Angeles Times*, August 9, 1983.
4. Peter Bunzel, "The Loud Family Attracts Television Limelight Again," *Los Angeles Herald Examiner*, August 1983, C1; Tom C. Smucker, "A Typical TV Family," *Village Voice*, August 30, 1983, 59.
5. Richard Stengel, "Looking in on the Louds," *Time*, August 22, 1983, 74; John Corry, "TV: The Louds Ten Years Later," *New York Times*, August 11, 1983, 1.
6. Stephen Reddicliffe, "*American Family Revisited:* Louds Older, Wiser 10 Years Later," *Dallas Times Herald*, August 1983; Arthur Unger, "Cable Documentary Tests the Boundaries of TV and 'Real Life,'" *Christian Science Monitor*, August 9, 1983.
7. Peggy Ziegler, "TV Fame and Its Effects: Checking in with the Louds," *Multichannel News*, August 22, 1983.
8. James Day, *The Vanishing Vision: The Inside Story of Public Television* (Berkeley: University of California Press, 1995).
9. Vito Russo, *The Celluloid Closet: Homosexuality in the Movies*, rev. ed. (New York: Harper & Row, 1987), 221–22.
10. Quoted in Steven D. Stark, *Glued to the Set: The 60 Television Shows and Events That Made Us Who We Are Today* (New York: Free Press, 1997), 170. As Stark points out, in the late 1980s, small video camcorders became part of everyday life, and amateur footage found its way onto news shows, weather reports, and entertainment programs, in particular *America's Funniest Home Videos* (1990–present), which presents family life as a slapstick comedy of errors. While *Cops* (1989–present) adapted the handheld verité shooting style to reality programming, *Unsolved Mysteries* (1988–1999) and *America's Most Wanted* (1988–present) continued to blend actuality footage with reenactments in ways that further confound distinctions between fiction and reality, entertainment and news.
11. Quoted in Stark, *Glued to the Set*, 279. In the interim, dysfunctional families have, of course, become a staple of television situation comedies such as *The Simpsons* (1989–present).
12. Albert Brooks worked on *The Great American Dream Machine* (1971–72) at NET in the early 1970s, while Gilbert was producing *An American Family*.
13. More recently, Hollywood filmmakers have further explored the invasion of everyday life by TV in works such as *The Truman Show* (Peter Weir, 1998), *Pleasantville* (Gary Ross, 1998), and *EDtv* (Ron Howard, 1999). These comic versions only slightly exaggerate the merger of reality and representation. In 1997, a Pennsylvania college student, Jennifer Ringley, set up a digital camera to take a picture of her dorm room every three minutes; the images captured by the "JenniCam" were then broadcast over the Internet twenty-four hours a day.
14. MTV's *The Real World* (1992–present) probably best embodies the trend toward the "society of the spectacle." It is a postmodern, Generation X offspring of Gilbert's series. Promoted as "the new American Family," *The Real World* effectively abolishes boundaries between fiction and documentary by casting aspiring performers as its subjects; three musicians, a painter, a dancer, a model, and a poet shared the limelight in the first season. Dystopic science fiction films such as *Rollerball* (Norman Jewison, 1975) and *The Running Man* (Paul Michael Glaser, 1987) anticipated a society governed by spectacle and television. But *An American Family* also helped to inspire serious nonfiction filmmakers. In Britain, the BBC broadcast a twelve-part nonfiction series, *The Family*, in 1974, modeled on *An American Family*, pulling in an audience of seven to ten million each week. It, too, generated widespread controversy and was even denounced in the British Parliament. See Colin Young, "*The Family*," *Sight and Sound* 43, no. 4 (1974): 206–11. In 1976, PBS aired Paul Wilkes's *Six American Families*. This six-part documentary series offered a composite portrait of the American family along representative lines of race, ethnicity, income, region, and occupation. In 1992, the BBC broadcast *Sylvania Waters*, a weekly nonfiction series that chronicled a year in the life of an Australian family, also generating considerable controversy. Jennifer Fox's *An American Love Story*, a ten-hour nonfiction series broadcast on PBS in 1999, explored a year in the life of an interracial couple and their two children in Queens, New York.
15. Edward Pincus, "One Person Sync-Sound: A New Approach to Cinema Verite," *Filmmaker's Newsletter*, December 1972, 25.
16. Personal communication, Portland, Oregon, July 25, 1999.
17. Mark Rance, "Home Movies and Cinéma-vérité," *Journal of Film and Video* 38, nos. 3–4 (1986): 96.

Bibliography

Alexander, Shana. *The Feminine Eye*. New York: McCall, 1970.
———. "The Silence of the Louds." *Newsweek*, January 22, 1973, 28.
Allen, Robert C. *Speaking of Soap Operas*. Chapel Hill: University of North Carolina Press, 1985.
Altman, Rick. "The Technology of the Voice I." *Iris* 3, no. 1 (1985): 3–20.
———. "The Technology of the Voice II." *Iris* 4, no. 1 (1986): 107–18.
———. "Introduction." In *Sound Theory/Sound Practice*, edited by Rick Altman. New York: Routledge,
   Chapman, & Hall, 1992.
———. "Sound Space." In *Sound Theory/Sound Practice*, edited by Rick Altman, 46–64. New York:
   Routledge, Chapman, & Hall, 1992.
"An American Family." *America*, February 10, 1973, 111.
"An American Family." *Chicago Tribune*, January 11, 1973, 9.
"An American Family." *Newsweek*, January 15, 1973, 68.
"An American Family." *TV Guide*, January 6, 1973, A61.
"An American Family." *TV Guide*, January 13, 1973, A60.
"An American Family." *TV Guide*, February 3, 1973, A58.
"An American Family Revisited: The Louds Ten Years Later." *Variety*, August 17, 1983, 64.
"And Another American Family." *Chicago Tribune*, March 3, 1973, 17.
Aruffo, Nancy. "Letter to the Editor." *New York Times*, March 11, 1973, 99.
Atkins, Thomas R. *Frederick Wiseman*. New York: Monarch, 1976.
Barnouw, Erik. *Documentary: A History of the Non-Fiction Film*. New York: Oxford University Press,
   1974.
Beck, Bernard. "Ghost in the Family." *Society* 11 (1974): 78–81, 83.
Benson, Thomas, and Carolyn Anderson. "The Rhetorical Structure of Frederick Wiseman's *Model*."
   Journal Film and Video 36, no. 4 (1984): 30–40.
Blake, Richard. "Families: Loud and Clear." *America*, June 16, 1973, 558.
Blakely, Robert J. *To Serve the Public Interest: Educational Broadcasting in the United States*. Syracuse,
   N.Y.: Syracuse University Press, 1979.
Bluem, A. William. *Documentary in American Television: Form, Function, Method*. New York: Hastings
   House, 1965.
Boeth, Richard. "Connubial Blitz: It Was Ever Thus." *Newsweek*, March 12, 1973, 56.
Bordwell, David, Janet Staiger, and Kristin Thompson. *The Classical Hollywood Cinema: Film Style
   and Mode of Production to 1960*. New York: Columbia University Press, 1985.
Bringuier, Jean-Claude. "Libres propos sur le cinéma-vérité." *Cahiers du Cinéma* 25 (July 1963): 16.
"The Broken Family: Divorce U.S. Style." *Newsweek*, March 12, 1973, 47–48, 50, 55, 57.
Broughton, Irv, ed. *Producers on Producing: The Making of Film and Television*. Jefferson, N.C.:
   McFarland, 1986.
Brown, Erica. "*An American Family*: Alive on the Screen." *Vogue*, January 1973, 68.
Brown, Les. *Television: The Business behind the Box*. New York: Harcourt Brace Jovanovich, 1971.
Bunzel, Peter. "The Loud Family Attracts Television Limelight Again." *Los Angeles Herald Examiner*,
   August 1983, C-1.
Carlin, Sybil. "Seeing the Loud Family." *Village Voice*, March 1, 1973, 15.
———. "Louds Sink Slowly in the West." *Village Voice*, April 5, 1973, 38.
———. "Bye, Patty. Bye, Bill. Bye, Margaret." *Village Voice*, April 12, 1973, 25.

Carroll, Noël. "From Real to Reel: Entangled in Nonfiction Film." *Philosophic Exchange* 14 (1983): 5–45.

———. *Mystifying Movies: Fads and Fallacies of Contemporary Film Theory.* New York: Columbia University Press, 1988.

Conn, F. M. "Letter to the Editor." *Commentary,* October 1973, 16.

Corry, John. "TV: The Louds Ten Years Later." *New York Times,* August 11, 1983, 1.

———. "Ten Years Later, the Once-Famous Loud Family Is Quieter." *Chicago Tribune,* August 17, 1983, 3.

Crook, David. "The Louds Revisited—on Pay TV." *Los Angeles Times,* August 9, 1983.

Day, James. "Something Rather Different: THIRTEEN's First Twenty-five Years." In *WNET Thirteen Retrospective: 25 Years on the Air,* 10–21. New York: Museum of Broadcasting, 1988.

———. *The Vanishing Vision: The Inside Story of Public Television.* Berkeley: University of California Press, 1995.

"The Divorce of the Year." *Newsweek,* March 12, 1973, 48–49.

Donohue, John W. "Afterthoughts on *An American Family.*" *America,* April 28, 1973, 390.

Dyer, Richard. *Heavenly Bodies: Film Stars and Society.* New York: St. Martin's, 1986.

Edelstein, David. "A Date with History." *Village Voice,* September 9, 1985.

Ellis, John. *Visible Fictions: Cinema, Television, Video.* London: Routledge & Kegan Paul, 1982.

Feuer, Jane. "Genre Study and Television." In *Channels of Discourse: Television and Contemporary Criticism,* edited by Robert C. Allen, 113–33. Chapel Hill: University of North Carolina Press, 1987.

Friedman, Jack. "Every Loud Has a Silver Lining." *Village Voice,* January 18, 1973, 59.

Gaines, Jim. "TV: The Decline and Fall of an American Family." *Saturday Review of the Arts,* January 1973, 47–48.

Geller, Robert. "Coming of Age in Santa Barbara: *An American Family.*" *Media and Methods,* March 9, 1973, 50–52.

Gilbert, Craig. "Reflections on *An American Family.*" *Studies in Visual Communication* 8, no. 1 (1982): 24–54.

———. "*An American Family*—the Credit Confusion." *New York Times,* October 18, 1994, A19.

Gilbert, Craig, and Susan Lester. "The Proposal." Unpublished WNET document, 1971.

Gorbman, Claudia. *Unheard Melodies: Narrative Film Music.* Bloomington: Indiana University Press, 1987.

Goulart, Ron, ed. *An American Family.* New York: Warner Paperback Library, 1973.

Gronbeck, Bruce E. "The Academic Practice of Television Criticism." *Quarterly Journal of Speech* 74 (1988): 334–47.

Hall, Jeanne Lynn. "Refracting Reality: The Early Films of Robert Drew and Associates." Ph.D. diss., University of Wisconsin-Madison, Department of Communication Arts, 1990.

Hamernick, Joseph M. "*Pat Loud: A Woman's Story.*" *Best Sellers,* May 1, 1974, 71.

Harrington, Stephanie. "*An American Family* Lives Its Life on TV." *New York Times,* January 7, 1973, 5.

———. "Of Loneliness and Publicity." *The Nation,* September 14, 1974, 219–20.

Hayakawa, S. I. "Can a Documentary Be Made of Real Life?" *Chicago Tribune,* March 11, 1973, 6.

Hindman, James, and Victoria Costello, eds. *The Independent Documentary: The Implications of Diversity, a Conference Report.* Washington, D.C.: American Film Institute, 1983.

Hoover, Dwight. *Middletown: The Making of a Documentary Film Series.* Philadelphia: Harwood, 1992.

Horowitz, Craig. "Reality Check." *People,* March 22, 1993, 61–63.

Hymes, Dell. "Models of the Interaction of Language and Social Life." In *Directions in Sociolinguistics,* edited by John J. Gumperz and Dell Hymes, 38–56. New York: Holt, Rinehart & Winston, 1972.

Jaffe, Patricia. "Editing Cinéma Vérité." *Film Comment* 3 (summer 1965): 43–47.

Junker, Howard, ed. *Salesman.* New York: Signet, 1969.

Kaplan, E. Ann. "Theories and Strategies of Feminist Documentary." In *New Challenges for Documentary,* edited by Alan Rosenthal, 78–102. Berkeley: University of California Press, 1988.

Kauffmann, Stanley. "Filming Filming." *New Republic,* April 1979, 24.

Kilday, Gregg. "The Rerun Life of Pat Loud." *Los Angeles Times,* May 2, 1974, 1, 14–15.

Kirsch, Robert. "Ross Macdonald: *The Underground Man.*" *Los Angeles Times,* March 14, 1971, 62.

———. "Pat Loud: A Part of the Age of Exposure." *Los Angeles Times,* April 28, 1974, 62.

Kozloff, Sarah. *Invisible Storytellers: Voice-Over Narration in American Fiction Film.* Berkeley: University of California Press, 1988.

Kramer, Carol. "Looking thru the Lens at One Man's Family." *Chicago Tribune,* February 1, 1973, 1–2.

———. "How the Louds Have Used the Limelight." *Chicago Tribune,* March 25, 1973, 1.

Krueger, Eric. "*An American Family:* An American Film." *Film Comment* 9 (November–December 1973): 16–19.

Levin, G. Roy. *Documentary Explorations: 15 Interviews with Film-Makers.* New York: Doubleday, 1971.

Leyda, Jay. *Films Beget Films.* New York: Hill & Wang, 1964.

Liebes, Tamar, and Elihu Katz. *The Export of Meaning: Cross Cultural Readings of "Dallas."* New York: Oxford University Press, 1990.

Loud, Pat. "Some Second Thoughts from *An American Family.*" *Los Angeles Times*, March 4, 1973, 7.

Loud, Pat, with Nora Johnson. *Pat Loud: A Woman's Story.* New York: Coward, McCann & Geoghegan, 1974.

———. *Pat Loud: A Woman's Story.* New York: Bantam, 1974.

"The Loud Family Attracts Television Limelight Again." *Los Angeles Herald Examiner*, August 9, 1983.

Lueloff, Jorie. "Materfamilias: Another Close (Off-Screen) Look at Pat Loud." *Chicago Tribune*, March 24, 1974, 3.

Mabley, Jack. "There Goes the Case for Gay Liberation." *Chicago Tribune*, March 25, 1973, 4.

Macdonald, Ross. *The Underground Man.* Boston: G. K. Hall, 1971.

MacDougall, David. "Beyond Observational Cinema." In *Principles of Visual Anthropology*, edited by Paul Hockings, 109–24. The Hague: Mouton, 1975.

Mamber, Stephen. *Cinema Verite in America: Studies in Uncontrolled Documentary.* Cambridge: MIT Press, 1974.

Marie, Michel. "Direct." In *Anthropology-Reality-Cinema: The Films of Jean Rouch*, edited by Mick Eaton, 35–39. London: British Film Institute, 1979.

McCarthy, Abigail. "*An American Family* and *The Family of Man.*" *Atlantic*, July 1973, 72–76.

Mead, Margaret. "As Significant as the Invention of Drama or the Novel." *TV Guide*, January 6, 1973, A61–63.

Mehta, Ved. *The Photographs of Chachaji: The Making of a Documentary Film.* New York: Oxford University Press, 1980.

Melville, Keith. *Marriage and Family Today.* New York: Random House, 1977.

Menaker, Dan. "*An American Family.*" *Harper's*, March 1973, 98–99.

Miller, Merle. *On Being Different: What It Means to Be a Homosexual.* New York: Popular Library, 1971.

———. "Dear Pat, Bill, Lance, Delilah, Grant, Kevin and Michele." *Esquire*, May 1973, 239–40, 242.

Murray, Michael. "The Louds of Santa Barbara." *Commonweal*, March 23, 1973, 60–62.

———. *The Videotape Book: A Basic Guide to Portable TV Production for Families, Friends, Schools and Neighborhoods.* New York: Bantam, 1974.

Newcomb, Horace, and Robert S. Alley. *The Producer's Medium: Conversations with Creators of American TV.* New York: Oxford University Press, 1983.

Nichols, Bill. "The Voice of Documentary." *Film Quarterly* 36, no. 3 (1983): 17–30.

———. *Representing Reality: Issues and Concepts in Documentary.* Bloomington: Indiana University Press, 1991.

Nordheimer, Jon. "He Feels Like a Kid Again, but His American Family Is in Ruins." *New York Times*, March 1, 1974, 1.

———. "The Loud Family a Year Later: Scarred but Proud." *Chicago Tribune*, March 18, 1974, 1.

O'Connell, P. J. *Robert Drew and the Development of Cinema Verite in America.* Carbondale: Southern Illinois University Press, 1992.

O'Connor, John J. "TV: Arguments over *An American Family* Are Smothering Its Contents." *New York Times*, January 22, 1973, 3.

———. "TV: *An American Family* Is a Provocative Series." *New York Times*, January 23, 1973, 1.

———. "Mr. & Mrs. Loud, Meet the Bradys." *New York Times*, March 4, 1973, 19–20.

———. "And Then for Something Truly Different." In *WNET Thirteen Retrospective: Twenty-five Years on the Air*, 55–62. New York: Museum of Broadcasting, 1988.

Oldham, Gabriella. *First Cut: Conversations with Film Editors.* Berkeley: University of California Press, 1992.

"Pat Loud: A Woman's Story." *Christian Century*, April 10, 1974, 402.

"Pat Loud: A Woman's Story." *Christian Science Monitor*, March 27, 1974, F4.

Petersen, Clarence. "Loud Family May Be Broken—but It's Not Broke." *Chicago Tribune*, March 21, 1973, 1, 6.

———. "'We Were Very Naive about a Lot.'" *Chicago Tribune*, March 22, 1973, 1, 6.

———. "'We Haven't Changed,' Says *The Family's* Father." *Chicago Tribune*, March 23, 1973, 14.

Pfeffer, Susan Beth. "*Pat Loud: A Woman's Story.*" *Library Journal*, April 15, 1974, 1123.

Pincus, Edward. "One Person Sync-Sound: A New Approach to Cinema Verite." *Filmmaker's Newsletter*, December 1972, 24–30.

Rabiger, Michael. *Directing the Documentary.* Boston: Focal Press, 1987.

Rance, Mark. "Home Movies and Cinéma-vérité." *Journal of Film and Video* 38, nos. 3–4 (1986): 95–98.

Raymond, Alan, and Susan Raymond. "Filming *An American Family.*" *Filmmaker's Newsletter*, March 6, 1973, 19–21.

———. "*An American Family.*" *American Cinematographer*, May 1973, 590–93, 604–5.

"Real-Life Louds Recall Their Days as TV's Louds." *Chicago Tribune*, April 22, 1973, 2.

Reddicliffe, Stephen. "American Family Revisited: Louds Older, Wiser 10 Years Later." *Dallas Times Herald*, August 1984.

Reich, Charles A. *The Greening of America.* New York: Bantam, 1970.

The Reminiscences of Alan and Susan Raymond. New York: Oral History Collection of Columbia University, 1980.

Rich, Frank. "The Gay Decade." *Esquire*, November 1987.

Rock, Gail. "All in a Real Family." *Ms.*, February 1973, 22–23.

Roiphe, Anne. "*An American Family*: Things Are Keen but Could Be Keener." *New York Times Magazine*, February 18, 1973, 8–9, 41, 45–46, 50–53.

———. "Ma and Pa and John Boy in Mythic America: *The Waltons*." *New York Times Magazine*, November 18, 1974, 40ff.

Rosenblatt, Roger. "Residuals on *An American Family*." *New Republic*, November 23, 1974, 20–24.

Rosenthal, Alan. *The New Documentary in Action: A Casebook in Film Making*. Berkeley: University of California Press, 1971.

Roszak, Theodore. *The Making of a Counterculture: Reflections on the Technological Society and Its Youthful Opposition*. New York: Doubleday, 1969.

Ruby, Jay. "The Image Mirrored: Reflexivity and the Documentary Film." *Journal of the University Film Association* 29, no. 4 (1977): 3–13.

———. "Exposing Yourself: Reflexivity, Film, and Anthropology." *Semiotica* 30, nos. 1–2 (1980): 153–79.

———. "Ethnography as Trompe L'Oeil: Film and Anthropology." In *A Crack in the Mirror: Reflexive Perspectives in Anthropology*, edited by Jay Ruby, 121–32. Philadelphia: University of Pennsylvania Press, 1982.

———. "Speaking for, Speaking about, Speaking with, or Speaking Alongside: An Anthropological and Documentary Dilemma." *Journal of Film and Video* 44, nos. 1–2 (1992): 42–66.

Russo, Vito. *The Celluloid Closet: Homosexuality in the Movies*. Rev. ed. New York: Harper & Row, 1987.

"Sample of One?" *Time*, February 26, 1973, 51–52.

Sanborn, Sara. "*An American Family*." *Commentary*, May 1973, 78–80.

———. "Sara Sanborn Writes." *Commentary*, October 1973, 16, 20.

Schopen, Bernard. *Ross Macdonald*. Boston: Twayne, 1990.

Sharbutt, Jay. "The Drama of TV's Last Real (?) Family." *Chicago Tribune*, February 27, 1973, 9.

Silverstone, Roger. *Framing Science: The Making of a BBC Documentary*. London: British Film Institute, 1985.

Singer, Mark. "Predilections." *New Yorker*, February 6, 1989.

Skolnick, Arlene. *Embattled Paradise: The American Family in an Age of Uncertainty*. New York: Basic Books, 1991.

Smith, Cecil. "Finding—and Filming—an American Family." *Los Angeles Times*, January 11, 1973, 1, 22.

———. "The Louds, 10 Years After . . . ." *Los Angeles Times*, August 11, 1983, VI-1.

Smucker, Tom C. "A Typical TV Family." *Village Voice*, August 30, 1983, 59.

"Spy Drama." *The Nation*, March 5, 1973, 293.

Staiger, Janet. *Interpreting Films: Studies in the Historical Reception of American Cinema*. Princeton, N.J.: Princeton University Press, 1992.

Stark, Steven D. *Glued to the Set: The 60 Television Shows and Events That Made Us Who We Are Today*. New York: Free Press, 1997.

Stengel, Richard. "Looking in on the Louds." *Time*, August 22, 1983, 74.

Taylor, Ella. *Prime-Time Families: Television Culture in Postwar America*. Berkeley: University of California Press, 1989.

Terry, John. "An American Family in Super-8." *Filmmaker's Newsletter*, March 6, 1973, 22–23.

"Ultimate Soap Opera." *Time*, January 22, 1973, 36.

Unger, Arthur. "Cable Documentary Tests the Boundaries of TV and 'Real Life.'" *Christian Science Monitor*, August 9, 1983.

Vaughan, Dai. "The Aesthetics of Ambiguity." In *Film as Ethnography*, edited by Peter Ian Crawford and David Turton, 99–115. Manchester: Manchester University Press, 1992.

Voeller, Bruce. "Letter to the Editor." *New York Times Magazine*, March 4, 1973, 4.

Ward, Melinda. "The Making of *An American Family*." *Film Comment* 9 (November–December 1973): 24–31.

———. "Pat Loud: An Interview." *Film Comment* 9 (November–December 1973): 20–23.

Waters, Harry F. "Wiseman's *Near Death*." *Newsweek*, January 22, 1990, 52.

Wilkes, Paul. *Six American Families*. New York: Parthenon, 1977.

Wilkinson, Rupert. *The Pursuit of American Character*. New York: Harper & Row, 1988.

WNET. "Background Production Information." In *An American Family* press packet, 1973.

———. "Episodes." In *An American Family* press packet, 1973.

———. "The Family." In *An American Family* press packet, 1973.

———. "Press Release." In *An American Family* press packet, 1973.

———. "Profile of the William C. Loud Family." In *An American Family* press packet, 1973.

Wood, Robin. "Rules of the Game." In *International Dictionary of Films and Filmmakers*, edited by Christopher Lyons, 389–91. New York: Perigree, 1985.

Woods, Crawford. "The Louds." *New Republic,* March 24, 1973, 23.

Worth, Sol. *Studying Visual Communication.* Edited by Larry Gross. Philadelphia: University of Pennsylvania Press, 1981.

Young, Colin. *"The Family." Sight and Sound* 43, no. 4 (1974): 206–11.

Zheutlin, Barbara. "The Politics of Documentary: A Symposium." In *New Challenges for Documentary,* edited by Alan Rosenthal, 227–44. Berkeley: University of California Press, 1988.

Ziegler, Peggy. "TV Fame and Its Effects: Checking in with the Louds." *Multichannel News,* August 22, 1983.

Intercviews

All interviews were conducted and tape-recorded by the author.

Carey, Alice. August 1, 1989.

Day, James. June 8, 1989.

Donnet, Jacqueline. June 1, 1989.

Gilbert, Craig. January 4, 1989; August 23, 1993.

Goodwin, Tom. July 24, 1991.

Hanser, David. June 2, 1989.

Lester, Susan. June 8, 1989.

Loud, Lance. June 10, 1990.

McElwee, Ross. March 17, 1988.

Negroponte, Michel. June 15, 1988.

Raymond, Alan. July 20, 1993.

Raymond, Alan, and Susan Raymond. August 8, 1989; March 16, 1994.

Terry, John. March 14, 1988.

Index

releases, 96–100, 131; characterized in reviews, 100–105; chosen for *An American Family*, 15–20; and Christmas, 67–68; composition of, 17–18, 30–31; criticizes cutting of *An American Family*, 118–19; criticizes TV, 107; a day in the life, 64–68, 71, 72–73, 76; and decline of American family, 113–15; described initially, 18–19; discusses the program, xviii; editorial control, 26–27; fan mail, 110, 126–27; finances, 71–72; goals, 114; influence of camera on, 117–18; interpret their representation, 120; living with, 40; the marriage, xvi, xviii, xxiii, 17, 19, 22, 35–36, 46, 48, 50, 59, 60, 63, 64, 66–67, 68–69, 72, 74–75, 81–82, 84, 87, 90, 99–100, 101, 105, 110, 111, 112, 113–14, 116, 118, 121, 127; perceived as invented, 106, 113, 115, 126; profiled on *An American Family*'s anniversaries, 130–31; public identifies with, 105; reacts to *An American Family*, 120–29; referential readings focused on, 107; retrospective criticism, xxiv, 130–37; as stars, xviii; transformed into celebrities, 37, 38; viewed as authors of *An American Family*, 103–4; viewed as symbol, 112

Loud, Bill: and his business, xxiii, 21, 61; criticizes *An American Family*, 120, 122; and game show host, xviii; and Grant Loud, 59; marriage proposals, 127; and Pat's autobiography, 122; retires, 131; and Vietnam War, xxiii. *See also* Loud family

Loud, Delilah: appears on *The Dating Game*, xx; attacked in press as insensitive, 104; attitude to parents' divorce, 113; criticism of *An American Family*, 48; and dance class, 53, 61, 64, 72; marketing director, 131

Loud, Grant: as actor, 131; celebrity, 130; characterizes *An American Family*, 130; criticizes critics, 129; and father, 59; and music, 62; as nightclub singer, 143n.18; running away, 111; and success, 70–71; summer job, xxiii, 61–63

Loud, Kevin: business career, 131; business trip, xxiii; and the military, 111

Loud, Lance: addressing the audience, 90–91; Andy Warhol fan, xviii; becomes freelance writer, 131; and Chelsea Hotel, 46, 58; described, 69; describes experience of being filmed, 24; in Europe, xxiii; fame, 120; forms punk rock music group Mumps, 143n.18; gay character on TV, xvi, xviii; gay symbol, xviii; and homosexuality, 127–28; his last word about *An American Family*, 131; his lifestyle, 100–101; in New York City, xxiii; out of the closet, 111, 127–28; overdubbing, 46; poses for *Screw*, xx; presence of camera, 29–30; and press attacks on homosexuality, 104–5; receives fan mail, 127; and his travels, 62–63; viewed as an invented character, 106

Loud, Michele: career, 131; and dance class, 53, 61

Loud, Pat: her autobiography, xviii–xix, 18, 25; becomes friends with Susan Lester, 30; claims loss of dignity, 126; complains about advertisements, 101; compliments *An American Family* staff, 120; criticizes Craig Gilbert, 121; description of, 22; gossip about, xviii, 116; lead char-

acter in *An American Family*, 59–60; life, 17; and her mother, 58; objects to editorial aspects of *An American Family*, 47; *Pat Loud: A Woman's Story*, xviii–xix, 18, 25, 30, 48, 122, 123–25; 126; previews *An American Family* episodes, 48; her travels, xxiii; the years after *An American Family*, 131

Louisiana Story, 56

Lovelace, Linda, 131

Lowe, David, 96

Lowell Thomas Remembers, 7

Mabley, Jack: editorial on *An American Family*, 128

MacDonald, Ross, 123, 125; influence on *An American Family*, 72; *The Underground Man* and Gilbert's idea of family, 17–18, 116

Madonna, 83

Magazine of the Arts, 8

Mailer, Norman: film influence, 4

Making of a Counterculture, The, xii, 13

Mamber, Stephen, 82

Mann, Anthony, 79

March of Time, The, 6, 8

Margaret Mead's New Guinea Journal, 9–11. *See also* Mead, Margaret

Marie, Michael, 80

Married Couple, A, 9, 12, 57, 106

Marshall, John, 142n.9

Mary Tyler Moore Show, The, xii, 14; compared to *An American Family*, 132–33

Maynard, Frederick: review of *An American Family*, 96

Maysles brothers [Albert and David], 3, 4, 11, 24, 38, 39, 106, 109; and independent documentaries, 56; and observational style, 55; and references to filmmaking within a film, 90; and use of musicians, 82

Mazursky, Paul: influenced by *An American Family*, xxv

McBride, Fern: NET producer, 10

McBride, Jim, 11, 57

McCarthy, Abigail: reviews *An American Family*, xviii, 112, 126, 127; writes autobiography, 108

McCarthy, Eugene, 107

McElwee, Ross, xxii; filming documentary, 33; parodist, 79; post-verité documentary, 79, 136

Mead, Margaret, 14, 108; autobiography, *Blackberry Winter*, 108; and documentary TV, 9–11; Gilbert's documentary, 9–10; *Margaret Mead's New Guinea Journal*, 9–11; name used in *An American Family* press packets, 102; praises *An American Family*, xv, xvii–xviii; reviewer of *An American Family*, 127; use of visual media, 9–10

Mecklinberg, Albert, 141–42n.34; sound technician, 36, 37

Media and Methods, 109

Mehta, Ved: and conventional filming, 27–28

Menaker, Daniel: *New Yorker* editor, xviii; reviews *An American Family*, 117

Microphones, 31; BS-II preamp, 32; omnidirectional, 31–32; Sennheiser 805 shotgun, 31; Sony

ECM-16, 31–32; taps, 31–32; Vega wireless lavaliere, 31, 32
Middletown: The Making of a Documentary Film Series, 147n.6
Mike Douglas Show, The: Louds appear on, xvii, 120
Miller, Arthur, 109, 114
Miller, Merle, xv; reviews *An American Family*, xviii, 100
Minolta Autospot light meter, 32–33
Model, 65, 84
Mom, 134
Monterey Pop, 82–83
Monterey Pop Festival, 82
Moore, Michael: and post-verité documentary, 79
Morin, Edgar: film director, 80; sociologist, 144n.37
Ms., 102, 127
Multichannel News, 131
Multiple characters, 59–63
Murray, Michael: director, xviii; reviews *An American Family*, 103, 106–7, 114, 123, 145n.41
Museum of Modern Art: first official press screening of *An American Family*, 50
Music, 82–86; in *An American Family*, xxiii, 84, 85–86; bridging sequences, 53; innovation in technology, 82–83; and observational style, 82; and Richard Rodgers, 55
My Left Foot, 11

Nagra tape recorders, 31, 32
Naked City, The, 79
Nana, Mom and Me, 134
Nanook of the North, 111
Narrative. See Observational style
Narrative omniscience: and *An American Family*, 53
Nation, The: reviews *An American Family*, xviii, 102, 106, 107, 108; reviews *An American Family* press packet, 108; reviews Pat Loud's autobiography, 123
Near Death, 126
Negroponte, Michel, 33–34
NET: and *An American Family* problems, 47; organizational hierarchy, 8; and public broadcasting, 5
Network TV: commercial, 5
New Green Revolution, The? 27–28
New Republic, The: critiques *An American Family*, xviii, 62, 102, 106
New York Post: reviews Pat Loud's autobiography, 123
New York Times: critiques *An American Family Revisited*, 130, 131; reviews *An American Family*, 103, 109–10, 116
New York Times Magazine, xv; *An American Family* advertised in, 98; *An American Family* discussed, xviii, 112–13; *An American Family* reviewed, xvi; Anne Roiphe reviews *An American Family*, 88, 100–104, 123; Lance Loud and homosexuality, 127–28
New Yorker: cartoon reproduced, 121; response to *An American Family*, 120

Newsday: reviews *An American Family Revisited*, 130
Newsweek: Louds on cover, xviii, 113; reports on Lance, 120; reviews *An American Family*, xv, xviii, 101, 103, 105, 110, 115; reviews Wiseman film *Near Death*, 126
Nichols, Bill, 96, 111, 112
Nichols, Mike, 90
Night Mail, 82
Nizo S56 camera, 36
Nonfiction series, xi–xii

O'Connor, John J., 100, 110, 116
Obenhaus, Marc, 85
Observational style, 54–58; and *An American Family*, xxii, xxiii, 53; and Andy Warhol, 56–57; and classical Hollywood cinema, 50–51; and dealing with the past, 88–89; departure from convention, 27–28; development of, 3; deviations from in *An American Family*, 86–87; difficulty, 33–34; editing techniques, 44–45; and Gustave Flaubert, 50; and impersonal narration, 89; interactions, 29, 30, 34–37; narrative, 53–54; and quantitative detail, 102; publicity negates, 98, 100; reaches mass audience for first time with *An American Family*, 109; and Roberto Rossellini, 57; and sound effects, 45–46; transformed by sound techniques, 78; tensions of, 65–66; and use of music, 82; use of sound, 77
Ochs, Phil, 8
omnidirectional microphones, 31–32
On Being Different, 100–101
On the Pole, 114
One Day at a Time, 68; influenced by *An American Family*, xxv, 132
Oprah Winfrey Show, The, xii; compared to *An American Family*, 133
Ordinary People: influenced by *An American Family*, xxv
Our Town, 66

Parry, David, 136
Partridge Family, The, 67, 112
Pat Loud: A Woman's Story: discussed, 123–25; fee for, 122
Paxton, Tom, 8
Pennebaker, D. A., 8; and Drew Associates, 50, 55–56; documentary auteur, 6; *Don't Look Back*, 3; use of music, 82–83
People: profiles Loud family twenty years later, 130; reviews *An American Family Revisited*, 130
Peyton Place, 112
Phil Donahue Show, The: Louds appear on, xvii, 120
Photographs of Chachaji, The: The Making of a Documentary Film: and conventional practice, 27–28
Picasso, Pablo, 8
Pilafian, Peter, 36
Pincus, Ed, xii, 134, 135, 136
Police Tapes, The, 131

Watt, Harry, 82
We Get Married Twice, 134
Wealth: as theme of *An American Family*, 102
Welfare, 65
Werner, Ken, 39, 42
What's Happening! The Beatles in the U.S.A., 56, 82–83
Who, The, 85–86
Who's Afraid of Virginia Woolf? TV competition, xv, 112
Wiesel, Elie, abjures TV, xv
Wilder, Thornton, 66
Wilkes, Paul: produces *Six American Families*, 16
Wilkinson, Rupert, 113
Williams, William Carlos, 8
Wiseman, Frederick, 8, 11; and Andy Warhol, 90; career summarized, 142n.9; and color film, 32; compared to Gilbert, 132; editorial control, 26–27; and film stars, 125–26; *High School*, 9, 65; institutional documentaries, 3, 6, 15, 16, 17, 26–27; and music copyright owners, 83–84, 85; narrative structure, 57; nonfiction film, 109; observational style, 89; and parody of music documentary, 83, 143n.1; support, 142n.45; use of American language, 79, 81
With Love from Truman: A Visit with Truman Capote, 4, 142n.38
WNET, 4, 21, 36, 37, 39, 50; and fate of *An American Family*, 6; press releases, xxiv; publicity campaign for *An American Family*, 96–102, 126
Wolfe, Tom: film influence, 4
Wolper, David, 82
Women's movement, 134; and Pat Loud, xviii
Woods, Crawford, 106, 123

Yasui, Lise, 136–37
Year in the Life, A: influenced by *An American Family*, xxv
Yeats, William, 113
Young, Colin, 111–12

Zavattini, Cesare, 56
Ziegler, Peggy, 131
Zwerin, Charlotte: documentary director, 142n.38; film cutter, 38, 39, 142n.38

JEFFREY RUOFF is a film historian, a documentary filmmaker, and assistant professor of film and television at Dartmouth College. He is the director of *The Last Vaudevillian, Forty Days across America*, and *Works of Art and Enid*, and the codirector of *Hacklebarney Tunes: The Music of Greg Brown*. He is also the coauthor of *The Emperor's Naked Army Marches On*.